D1766629

SHEFFIELD WEDNESDAY
Miscellany

SHEFFIELD WEDNESDAY
Miscellany

*Owls Trivia,
History, Facts & Stats*

JASON DICKINSON

SHEFFIELD WEDNESDAY
Miscellany

All statistics, facts and figures are correct as of 5th May 2010

© Jason Dickinson

Jason Dickinson has asserted his rights in accordance with the Copyright, Designs and Patents Act 1988 to be identified as the author of this work.

Published By:
Pitch Publishing (Brighton) Ltd
A2 Yeoman Gate
Yeoman Way
Durrington
BN13 3QZ

Email: info@pitchpublishing.co.uk
Web: www.pitchpublishing.co.uk

First published 2010

A catalogue record for this book is available from the British Library.

10-digit ISBN: 1-9054116-6-9
13-digit ISBN: 978-1-9054116-6-5

Printed and bound in Malta by Gutenberg Press

In Memory of

Corporal Liam Matthew Riley (1988-2010)

& John Eastwood Junior (1988-2006)

Forever Wednesday

ACKNOWLEDGEMENTS

I would like to express my thanks to all those at Pitch Publishing, most notably Dan Tester who has guided me through the various stages that eventually result in a book hitting the shelves. A big thank you to Mel Sterland for penning the foreword and also thanks to Sheffield Wednesday for giving their permission for the official badge to adorn the cover of this publication, and particularly to Trevor Braithwait, Colin Wood and Sue Evans at the club for their help. In addition, thanks to Michelle, my wife, for her love and understanding as I spent countless nights in my office writing this follow up to *Sheffield Wednesday On This Day*. Finally, thanks to friends, and fellow Wednesday fans, Mick Grayson, Pete Law, Stuart Laver and Roger Strain who have searched their memory banks for several of the subjects that have been covered in the book – helping the time pass on those long away trips!

FOREWORD BY MEL STERLAND

It was my brother, Terry, who first took me to watch Wednesday and I would stand on the Kop dreaming that one day it would be me running around in the blue and white shirt. It was while playing as a centre forward in Sheffield junior football that I was spotted by Wednesday scouts and invited to train at the club. Before long, I was turning out for the Owls' nursery side, Middlewood Rovers, and my dream came closer when, aged 15, I signed schoolboy forms. During my time as a £26 a week apprentice I was, like my fellow trainees, expected to undertake all sorts of chores, such as scrubbing the baths, cleaning the boots of the senior professionals and even painting the stands during the close season. If you did not do your job right you certainly knew about it, getting a telling off or a clip around the ear to make sure you did better next time!

I was still an apprentice when I was named as a substitute for the home game against Blackpool in May 1979 and was frightened to death when I replaced Brian Hornsby in the 78th minute! Although the crowd was only about 7,000 it seemed like 70,000 to me. In a practice match, on the following day, I was included in the first team against the reserves and it was a great feeling to realise I could be playing in the final home game of the season, against Hull City. I was duly included in the starting line up and the day became even more memorable when I crashed the ball into the net with my right foot – my dad was particularly pleased as he had placed a bet that I would score! In my early years at Wednesday I was mainly used in a midfield role, to not much acclaim, but the break my career needed came in September 1981 when our regular right-back, Ray Blackhall, was injured in the warm-up and I replaced him in the side. From that point I never looked back and became a first team regular with fans handing me the nickname of 'Zico', after the Brazilian superstar of the time (although Jack Charlton called me the 'flying pig').

Training became a lot tougher when Howard Wilkinson took over in 1983 but it paid immediate dividends as Wednesday won promotion back to the First Division after a 14-year absence – I was lucky enough to score the winning penalty that helped us to beat Crystal Palace 1-0 at Hillsborough, to clinch promotion. I also scored from the spot in our first game back in the First Division – a memorable 3-1 Hillsborough win over Forest – and netted again in the final minute of an astonishing 4-4 League Cup draw with Chelsea; a match we threw away after leading 3-0 at the break. I enjoyed playing under both Charlton and Wilkinson – for very different reasons – although it was always difficult every Monday morning, when 'Wilko' was in charge, not to exceed my target weight of 13 stones 2 lbs – it was in my contract that I would be fined £100 for every pound I was over at the weekly weigh in!

I was heartbroken to lose in two FA Cup semi-finals with the Owls but 1988 proved a great year as I scored my best goal for Wednesday – a real solo effort against Arsenal. Later in the year I felt proud to win what proved to be my only full cap for England, in a friendly in Saudi Arabia. We flew to the game on Concorde and ate sirloin steak on the flight – not bad for a lad from the Manor! I was also proud to captain Wednesday on many occasions but when new manager, Peter Eustace, stripped me of the role I was gutted, eventually moving to Glasgow Rangers in February 1989 after failing to regain the captaincy. After a decade as a professional it was time to move on but I loved my time at Wednesday and they will always be my club – I hope you enjoy *Sheffield Wednesday Miscellany* and feel proud to support one of England's greatest clubs.

Mel Sterland
Sheffield Wednesday (1979-89)
49 goals in 347 games, 1 England cap

INTRODUCTION

Sheffield Wednesday Miscellany is simply that; a random collection of stories, statistics, records, long forgotten facts and comical events that have combined to give the Owls such a rich and fascinating history.

The book covers all the major events in the club's 140-plus-year history, although in some cases this could just be a story pertaining to a player's lucky charm or how a cup win was celebrated on the streets of Victorian Sheffield. Single games and whole seasons are reviewed, such as the great escape of 1927/28 or the tremendous day at Cardiff in 2005. The club's players also feature prominently, from the likes of Chris Waddle, Ron Springett and Martin Hodge, to the plethora of loan players that have pulled on the famous blue and white shirt; long forgotten men such as Bojan Djordjic, Adam Chambers and Con Blatsis.

For the statisticians out there, a few lists are also included – from all the club's managers and top scorers to Wednesday's best and worst start to a season. Also read about the original 'blind draw', the reason why several pounds of onions ruined a club trip to the theatre and even about a former player who was killed by a bolt of lightning! Hopefully, the book will delight fans of the club and raise a few smiles along the way – enjoy the read.

Jason Dickinson

TRAINSPOTTING – 1

During the 1930s, a total of 23 locomotives were built and named after some of the most famous football clubs in Britain. Wednesday were one such club, along with the likes of Tottenham Hotspur and Liverpool, with their named engine being built in 1936. After 23 years the loco was decommissioned, and subsequently dismantled, at Doncaster. However, the colourful brass nameplates were preserved and in a luncheon held at the Royal Victoria hotel in Sheffield, one was officially presented to Wednesday chairman, Dr Andrew Stephen, by British Railways manager Mr Sparks (obviously an electrical engineer!). The nameplate was immediately mounted over the entrance to the old South Stand and has remained on show to this day.

MUD, GLORIOUS MUD

Wednesday continued to pull away from the Third Division danger zone on April Fools' Day 1978 with a 1-0 win at Hereford United. The game, however, was played on an old fashioned mudbath of a pitch and fans back home read in the local press that Roger Wylde had snatched the winner after 78 minutes. Headlines such as 'Wonder Wylde' and 'Wylde lifts Wednesday' were probably disappointing for Ian Porterfield, as he had scored the winner! The players were so mud splattered that reporters had mistakenly given the goal to Wylde although this was corrected a few days after the match, ensuring Porterfield was officially credited with his first goal for Wednesday since signing from Sunderland in July 1977.

HIGHBURY HONEYMOON

Wednesday and England goalkeeper Ron Springett signed for the club in March 1958 but the move caused a headache for Ron, and his intended wife, as the couple were due to get married in London, on a Saturday, just nine days after he had joined the Owls! Thankfully, the fixture list proved kind to Springett as Wednesday were playing in the capital, at Arsenal, on the same day. All the players, secretary-manager Eric Taylor, trainer-coach Jack Marshall and director Mr Gardiner therefore swelled the wedding party considerably before they all rushed off to Highbury (Springett included) to face the Gunners in a First Division game. Unfortunately, Ron could not stop a 1-0 win for Arsenal to deepen Wednesday's woes at the foot of the table.

GLOBE TREKKERS

The 100th anniversary of the Owls' first game on foreign soil – in Gothenburg, Sweden in May 1911 – will be celebrated in 2011. In the ensuing 99 years, the club have played both competitive and non-competitive games in numerous countries, in both Europe and further afield:

Austria	1968, 2010
Belgium	1954
Bulgaria	1965, 1966
Canada	1987
Denmark	1911, 1934, 1935, 1936, 1946, 1950, 1964, 2002
Finland	1986, 1987
France	1935, 1954, 1961, 1968
Georgia	1960
Germany	1956, 1963, 1964, 1987, 1992, 1995
Greece	1992
Hong Kong	1966
Ibiza	2004
Italy	1961, 1970, 1990
Japan	1994
Kuwait	1986, 1988
Luxembourg	1992
Malaysia	1966
Malta	2009
Mexico	1967
Netherlands	1932, 1956, 1961-63, 1965, 1996, 1997, 2003, 2007, 2008
Nigeria	1961
Poland	1965
Republic of Ireland	1933, 1971, 1992, 1994, 1997
Russia	1960
Singapore	1966
South Africa	1992
Spain	1962, 1965, 1994
Sweden	1911, 1934, 1946, 1950, 1973, 1984, 1990, 2002
Switzerland	1929, 1952, 1995
Thailand	1985
United States	1991, 2006

STAND-IN GOALIE

The relatively recent arrival of the substitute goalkeeper has meant the sight of an outfield player donning the goalkeeping gloves is becoming increasingly rare. In pre-substitute days, clubs had no choice but to throw an outfield player between the sticks and hope he wouldn't leak too many goals! Wednesday have generally been lucky as the majority of goalie 'cameos' have resulted in positive results, with the emergency man often ending up as a hero. However, on the other side of the coin was the experience of defender Norman Curtis at Preston, in August 1953, who took over after just ten minutes when Dave McIntosh fractured his arm. Wednesday were already trailing to a first minute goal and poor old Curtis proceeded to let five goals into his net as North End completed a 6-0 victory. The most bizarre statistic, however, was that Curtis managed to save not one but TWO penalties! In March 1973, Peter Springett was forced off at the interval of the Hillsborough game with Brighton & Hove Albion and his replacement, Peter Eustace, was just seven minutes from keeping a clean sheet until the Seagulls grabbed a late equaliser. Replacement Dave Rushbury did manage to keep a second-half clean sheet in October 1978 when he donned the green jersey after Bob Bolder broke his right elbow in the 0-0 home meeting with Carlisle United. The last 20 years has seen David Hirst, Andy Booth and Lee Bullen grab the headlines for their exploits between the sticks. Hirst was pressed into service in January 1990 when Kevin Pressman suffered cruciate knee ligament damage in the home game against Manchester City. Wednesday were leading 1-0 but Nigel Pearson duly added a second as Hirsty kept a 28-minute clean sheet. The appearance of Booth came in extraordinary circumstances on the last day of the 1996/97 season after Kevin Pressman was injured 59 minutes into the Hillsborough Premiership meeting with Liverpool. His replacement, Matt Clarke, was then controversially sent off by David Ellery leaving Booth to put on the gloves for the remaining seven minutes. Unfortunately, the Reds scored immediately from the resultant free kick but Booth secured a point at the death when he managed to save a shot with his face! Arguably the most important contribution from an emergency custodian came from Lee Bullen in February 2006, during a relegation six-pointer at Millwall. He replaced the injured David Lucas just before the break and kept the Lions out while Frank Simek scored a highly contentious winner.

LEE BULLEN IN UNUSUAL POSE

THE GOAL THAT NEVER WAS

In only their second season in the FA Cup, Wednesday made the very short trip to Quibell's Field (near Hyde Park in Sheffield) to face local rivals Providence. The home side could only muster ten players for the November 1881 tie that saw Wednesday go ahead after an hour when Anthony's goal-bound shot was handled by a home player on his own goal-line. This was, however, the first and only season when a new rule change was in force, resulting in the goal being awarded to the away side despite the ball clearly having failed to cross the line!

THE LONGEST GAME – 1

During the club's pre-season tour of the United States in 2006, the Owls faced North Carolina-based Wilmington Hammerheads in the opening game. On the afternoon of the friendly the heat on the Cape Fear was stifling but conditions turned in the most dramatic way later in the evening as dark clouds rolled over the Legion Sports Ground. After the National Anthems had been played, and the cheerleaders performed their routines, the teams kicked off but after 37 minutes had elapsed all the players, officials and spectators ran for shelter as a violent electrical storm engulfed the area. Incredibly, after a delay of some 75 minutes, everybody (minus a few fans who had drifted off home) re-emerged and it was decided to forget about the rest of the first half and just play the final 45 minutes of the game. The fixture eventually finished 1-1 with the final whistle sounding almost three hours after the game had started!

PASS THE LETTER OPENER!

When the Owls reached the sixth round of the FA Cup in 1954, they invited postal applications for tickets to the impending quarter-final clash with Bolton Wanderers at Hillsborough. On Monday 1st March 1954, a staggering 29,000 letters were delivered to the ground as cup fever gripped the blue and white half of the city. A crowd of 65,000 packed into the old ground to see the game, which ended all square. The Owls won 2-0 at Bolton in a replay after the 1-1 draw in Sheffield. Wednesday eventually lost to Preston in the last-four meeting at Maine Road, Manchester.

WINS AND LOSSES

BIGGEST WINS

League

9-1 v Birmingham City	13/12/1930
8-0 v Sunderland	26/12/1911

FA Cup

12-0 v Halliwell	17/01/1891
12-1 v Spilsby	04/11/1882

League Cup

8-0 v Aldershot	03/10/1989
7-1 v Leicester City	27/10/1992

BIGGEST DEFEATS

League

10-0 v Aston Villa	05/10/1912
9-0 v Derby County	21/01/1899

FA Cup

6-1 v Blackburn Rovers	29/03/1890
5-0 v Everton	27/01/1988

League Cup

8-2 v Queens Park Rangers	06/11/1973
5-0 v Carlisle United	07/09/1971

GREAT ESCAPE – 1

With only six games remaining of the 1893/94 season, Wednesday found themselves in the bottom three. In the early 1890s, the bottom three in the First Division played the top three in the Second Division to decide relegation and promotion. These games were called 'test matches' but Wednesday avoided them, winning five consecutive games to finish 12th out of 16.

ONE NIGHT IN BANGKOK

When Wednesday and fellow First Division side Watford agreed to visit Bangkok in May 1985 it was lauded by the home association as somewhat of a coup. Unfortunately, the tour proved somewhat problematic for the English sides as poor and incompetent organisation dogged the arrangements from start to finish, initially causing Wednesday's first game, against Bangkok Bank, to be cancelled. Both sides then had no choice but to refuse to take the field for the televised 'showpiece' match until the tour promoters had coughed up at least 50% of the monies they had promised! With the match being televised live the cash was eventually forthcoming (the remaining half never materialised) but the sides then had to cope with another problem – it was the rainy season and the pitch at the Dan Daeng Stadium was covered in pools of water, up to two inches deep! The mud-splattered teams tried, manfully, to put on a display for the sparse crowd of around two thousand but the game ended 0-0 after 90 minutes, leaving the unnamed trophy to be decided on penalty kicks. Wednesday reserve keeper Iain Hesford proved to be the hero – first choice Martin Hodge had been injured on the first day of training in the Far East – as he saved from Nigel Callaghan and Steve Terry as the Owls clinched the win, 3-2 on spot kicks. Wednesday then spent a few days of rest and recuperation before flying home, no doubt wishing they would not be returning any time soon!

THE FIRST CUP

Just over six months after their formation, The Wednesday were one of four teams invited to compete for the newly introduced Cromwell Cup. The competition was the brainchild of the Sheffield Theatre Royal's actor-manager Oliver Cromwell and was open to clubs that had been in existence for less than two years. On a windy February day in 1868, Wednesday overcame Exchange Brewery 4-0 in the first semi-final while the Garrick club joined Wednesday in the final by defeating Wellington seven days later. The final was hard fought and finished 0-0 after both sides had gone close to breaking the deadlock. The teams then agreed to play on until a 'golden goal' was scored and it was the "Wednesday men and their friends" who were celebrating as the winning goal was scrimmaged into the Garrick net.

WAR OF THE MONSTER TRUCKS

The events of April 21st 1991 will forever be treasured by Wednesday fans who watched the Owls win their first major trophy since 1935. However, it was the events immediately after the League Cup final win over Manchester United that caused controversy in South Yorkshire and led directly to the launch of a new fanzine. After Ron Atkinson's Wednesday had won the trophy all the fans who had witnessed the triumph on TV sat back to lap up all the post-match celebrations (not forgetting the thousands at Wembley who had set their VCR for the historic moment). However, you could have heard a pin drop in Wednesdayite front rooms as Yorkshire TV, in their infinite wisdom, decided there would be no call for highlights and instead broadcast *War of the Monster Trucks*. The cries of derision and accusations of West Yorkshire bias for the Leeds-based TV station could almost be heard on Wembley Way as every ITV region in the country showed the post-match footage except the county of the winning team! It was an act that will never be forgiven by Wednesday fans and in 1993 the treachery was immortalised with the launch of the fanzine *War of the Monster Trucks*. Based at the New Barrack Tavern, near to the ground, the fans organ was edited by a legendary labrador – Sir Stanley Headfire, a fat stinky pooch. One night, he lay too close to the hearth fire after a run on the snowy Wadsley Common. Unfortunately, the steam from Stanley's wet fur soon turned to smoke and Stanley was only saved by the application of a full can of Stones Bitter. All Northern boys know that beer is mental food and as the liquid doused Stanley he turned into a superhero dog, possessing powers of communication and was immediately appointed as editor of *War of the Monster Trucks*. The first issue was launched soon after with the headline; 'Lucan Alive! Found in Sheffield United's Trophy Room.' Over the years that followed WOTMT became the desired read of discerning Owls fans as Stanley provided an irreverent look at all things blue and white. His many friends and acquaintances included the staff at the New Barrack Tavern (especially those who could provide tasty sausages), Paolo Di Canio's pet monkey and Frankie Frederick – a guinea pig with powers of exorcism! Suggestions that David Richards, Matthew Cooper and Paul Taylor were really running the show have been constantly denied by Sir Stanley!

EUROPEAN SCOUT

It is well known that Yugoslavian Ante Mirocevic was Wednesday's first 'foreign' signing in 1980 but two years earlier the club made concerted efforts to sign fellow Yugoslavian Mojas Radonjic. The forward played for the same club as Mirocevic – Buducnost of Titograd – and it was Wednesday coach Ian St. John who was given the rather unenviable task of travelling behind the 'Iron Curtain' to watch the transfer target in action. It would be a journey that the future TV presenter would certainly remember as his flight from Heathrow to Belgrade was first delayed by five hours due to fog, and then forced to land in Ljubljana, in modern-day Slovenia. It was then an overnight stay before more fog meant a mere seven-hour delay, meaning that when St. John finally arrived in Belgrade it was impossible to reach the place where Radonjic was playing! However, St. John was not to be beaten and with his target playing three days later, he took advantage of the unexpected gap in his trip to watch and train with Red Star Belgrade. Unfortunately, it was not possible to reach Tuzia – the venue of the Yugoslav's next game – by plane so the intrepid scout hired a car and driver and then spent a hazardous four hours navigating the mountain roads during a snowstorm. The car broke down ten miles from his destination and when St. John finally reached the ground he discovered his interpreter had failed to show. The game was played in terrible conditions but, thankfully, Radonjic did appear and suitably impressed the Wednesday representative to be invited back to Sheffield for a trial. He duly arrived in December 1978 but the irony of the whole saga was that the Owls failed to gain a work permit for the player nicknamed 'The Eagle' and the whole transfer collapsed like a deck of cards!

IT'S IN REF!

The Owls' fight against relegation in March 1958 looked to have received a boost when a terrific 14th-minute shot from Albert Quixall beat Manchester United goalkeeper, Harry Gregg, to put Wednesday ahead. However, while the 35,608 Hillsborough crowd were still cheering, the referee realised that the ball had actually entered the net through a rather large hole in the side netting! The visitors were lucky to escape but Wednesday still won the game, thanks to a Roy Shiner goal, but unfortunately did not avoid the drop, finishing bottom of the pile.

COUPON BUSTERS

Wednesday's fight against relegation in 2008 was helped (or hindered, depending upon your view) with a club record run of seven consecutive draws. The sequence started with a 0-0 draw at Coventry City on March 15th and Wednesday then drew 2-2 against Crystal Palace before sharing the points with Stoke City (1-1), Coventry City (1-1), Scunthorpe United (1-1), Sheffield United (2-2) and Plymouth Argyle (1-1) before losing 2-1 at Blackpool on April 19th.

WHAT'S IN A NAME – 1

In the early days of the club's history, they were simply known as 'The Wednesday FC'. This was, of course, the name of the cricket club from which the football branch grew in 1867. When Wednesday moved to their Olive Grove ground in 1887 the club built a stand that had the words 'Sheffield Wednesday' painted on the roof! Over the years that followed the club became increasingly referred to by their two-word moniker and finally, on August 3rd 1929, the name of the company was officially changed from The Wednesday FC to Sheffield Wednesday FC – hence the reason why the former won the league championship in 1929, and latter a year later!

CRICKET CLUB

At Norton Lees in August 1911, the football section of The Wednesday Club met the cricket section with players of the winter game scoring 132 runs to just 77 accrued by the summer players. The cricket club was, of course, formed before the football club, back in 1820, but was sadly disbanded in September 1924, mainly due to the fact that they did not have a home ground to call their own.

NOT AWAY AGAIN!

Between 1962 and 1966 Wednesday were drawn away from home in the FA Cup on ten consecutive occasions. The sequence started with a fourth round tie at Nottingham Forest in January 1962, and ended in January 1967 when QPR were beaten 3-0 at Hillsborough. Of course, the Owls famously reached Wembley in 1966 without playing a single tie at home.

HITMEN

The Owls' history is littered with goalscorers who have helped make Wednesday a force in the game. Record scorer, Scot Andrew Wilson, netted all 199 league goals in top-flight football and his tally is unlikely to be bettered. Second in the list, and the best total since the war, is Sheffield-born inside-forward John Fantham who surpassed the previous post-war record holder Red Froggatt with a flurry of top-flight goals in the 1960s. Sixth is David Hirst, who perhaps could easily have beaten Fantham to second place on the all-time list if injuries had not restricted his appearances in the latter years of his Owls career. Pre-war men Spiksley, Trotter, McLean and Chapman complete the '100 club'.

Andrew Wilson (1900-1920) 216
John Fantham (1956-1969) 166
Redfern Froggatt (1943-1962) 148
Ellis Rimmer (1928-1938) 140
Mark Hooper (1927-1939) 135
David Hirst (1986-1997) 128
Fred Spiksley (1891-1904) 115
Jimmy Trotter (1922-1930) 114
David McLean (1911-1919) 100
Harry Chapman (1899-1911) 100
Roy Shiner (1955-1959) 96
Jack Ball (1930-1933) 94
Jackie Sewell (1951-1955) 92
Alan Finney (1950-1966) 88
Jack Allen (1927-1931) 85
Lee Chapman (1984-1988) 78
Harry Burgess (1929-1935) 77
Dennis Woodhead (1945-1955) 75
Mark Bright (1992-1997) 70
Harry Davis (1900-1907) 67

TRUST IN ME

When 1980s midfielder Pat Heard ended his playing days he decided on a rather radical career change as, with the help of PFA funding, he retrained to become a hypnotist!

THE FIRST HISTORIAN

The modern-day supporter is somewhat spoilt with choice regarding printed matter on their favourite team. Club histories started to hit the shelves with increasing regularity from the 1980s and now the majority of league sides have been covered in print. However, before that explosion it was extremely rare to find such volumes on club football and virtually unheard of in pre-war days. Sheffield Wednesday was an exception to that rule. In August 1926, Richard A. Sparling published his seminal work on the club *The Romance of the Wednesday*. The fascinating work covered the club's early years in depth with Dick Sparling, who covered the Owls' games for the local press and later became sports editor at *The Star*, using his vast knowledge to publish a work that has became a real classic in the realms of sporting books. The complete works were reprinted in 1997, so his legacy could be read by a new generation of Owls fans. He passed away on March 16th 1972 in Sheffield.

WE PROTEST

During the late 19th century, it became the vogue for clubs to protest to the FA after they had been knocked out of the FA Cup, the appeal usually relating to the ineligibility of an opposition player. This was the case in January 1883 when Wednesday were drawn against Nottingham Forest in the third round of the 'English Cup'. Before the game in Nottingham, played at Trent Bridge, Forest claimed that Wednesday player Malpas had been paid thirty shillings to play for Sheffield Wanderers in a game at Bolton. This was upheld and with the Wednesday man 'cup-tied' the game was drawn 2-2. Before the reply, Forest captain Sam Widdowson went to extraordinary lengths in an attempt to launch another protest – he travelled to Sheffield to trawl through Wednesday's minute books and even plastered posters around the city advertising a £20 reward for evidence that any players were not genuine members of Wednesday! Wednesday won the Bramall Lane replay 3-2 although Forest played under protest, alleging the pitch was unfit. After losing they protested again, about eligibility of players, but the FA Committee eventually dismissed the claims and censured the Nottingham club. This farcical situation was finally stamped out in the early 1890s when the FA ruled that protests could only be lodged pre-match.

HOSPITAL HELP

The Owls' 2009 link-up with Sheffield Children's Hospital made positive headlines both locally and nationally but this was not the first time Wednesday had helped to raise funds for health care. All the way back in April 1911, the Owls played Hull City for the Hull Hospital Cup while in September 1932 Wednesday lost 3-1 at Huddersfield Town in a game played for the Huddersfield Infirmary Cup; the match raised £272 in old money – approximately £14,000 at today's prices. Either side of World War II, Wednesday were regular visitors to Scunthorpe to face their non-league hosts for the Scunthorpe Hospital Cup, appearing for the last time in 1950. The club also played for the Scarborough Hospital Shield in 1934 and the hospital nurses were not forgotten either – an Owls reserve side lost 5-3 at Clay Cross Town in April 1924 in a game to raise funds for the local nurses' association.

THE LONGEST GAME – 2

The Owls' First Division meeting with Aston Villa during the 1898/99 season earned a unique place in the history books of the English game: the Olive Grove match took almost four months to complete! It started in November 1898 and ended in March of 1899! The fixture was scheduled for November 26th 1898, but kicked off six minutes late as the appointed referee, Mr Scragg from Crewe, had missed his train and failed to show. Luckily, a member of Wednesday's committee – Mr Bye – was a recognised referee so he took the whistle until half-time, when the original official arrived. The game was being played in increasingly murky conditions; Wednesday led 2-1 at the break and added a further goal from Hemmingfield before light became so poor that the official made the rather brave decision to abandon the game with just over ten minutes remaining. However, that was not the end of the matter. At a subsequent Football League meeting it was decided that instead of replaying the full 90 minutes, the teams would be required to play only the final ten minutes! Therefore, and quite bizarrely, the teams reconvened at Olive Grove on March 13th 1899 where 3,000 fans were in attendance to see the final ten and a half minutes of play. Wednesday added a further goal to complete a 4-1 win. They then beat Villa 2-0 in a 35 minutes each way benefit game for home forward Harry Davis.

EARLY BIRDS

Most clubs advise their fans to take their seats at least 15 minutes prior to kick off; good advice when you consider that most football fans will testify that missing an early goal can cause mixed emotions – particularly if it's the only goal of the game. Over the years no fewer than 28 Owls players have caused that feeling of joy, tinged with disappointment, for Wednesday's late arriving fans. The following list of players have scored inside the opening minute for the club:

Charlie Tomlinson	12 secs	v Preston North End (a) 1-0	22/10/49
John Pearson	13 secs	v Bolton Wanderers (h) 3-1	07/09/82
Steve Bould (og)	15 secs	v Arsenal (h) 1-0	17/02/90
Mark Bright	22 secs	v Crewe Alex. (LC) (a) 2-2	06/10/92
Simon Donnelly	25 secs	v Portsmouth (h) 2-3	03/11/01
Jock Wright	30 secs	v Woolwich Arsenal (a) 2-1	11/11/99
Fred Spiksley	30 secs	v Wolves (n) 2-1	18/04/1896
Fred Spiksley	30 secs	v Small Heath (h) 1-2	19/04/02
George Robertson	30 secs	v Sunderland (h) 1-2	25/12/12
Harry Burgess	30 secs	v Sheffield United (a) 1-1	06/09/30
Charlie Napier	30 secs	v Manchester City (a) 1-1	26/04/39
Eddie Quigley	30 secs	v Grimsby Town (h) 4-1	16/10/48
Keith Ellis	30 secs	v Birmingham City (h) 3-0	29/04/57
Albert Quixall	30 secs	v Bristol Rovers (h) 3-1	06/09/58
John Fantham	30 secs	v Nottingham Forest (a) 2-1	01/10/60
Alan Mullery (og)	30 secs	v Fulham (a) 6-1	21/01/61
Bronco Layne	30 secs	v Ipswich Town (h) 3-1	07/09/63
Dave Rushbury	30 secs	v Brighton & HA (a) 2-3	03/05/77
Marcus Tudgay	30 secs	v Burnley (h) 4-1	09/08/08
Dennis Woodhead	35 secs	v Blackpool (a) 2-1	17/10/53
Imre Varadi	36 secs	v Blackpool (LC) (h) 3-1	12/10/88
Mike Lyons	38 secs	v Torquay U. (FAC) (a) 3-2	29/01/83
Alan Finney	40 secs	v Fulham (a) 2-1	28/12/59
Carl Shutt	44 secs	v Liverpool (a) 2-2	01/01/86
Tommy Spurr	46 secs	v Sheffield United (a) 2-1	07/02/09
Lee Chapman	47 secs	v Oxford United (a) 1-2	28/03/87
Denis Leman	50 secs	v Colchester United (a) 2-0	24/01/81
Paolo Di Canio	50 secs	v Newcastle United (h) 2-1	10/01/98
Garry Thompson	55 secs	v Orient (FAC) (h) 5-0	25/01/86

BORN IN THE USA

John Harkes was one of the most popular Wednesday players of recent times. The New Jersey-born player set many firsts in the English game, including the first US player to appear and score in a major Wembley final. He arrived at Wednesday on trial in January 1990 and eventually returned on loan eight months later, prior to signing from the US Soccer Federation for $185,000 in December 1990. It was during his loan spell that he scored a wonder goal in a 2-1 League Cup win at First Division Derby County, and before that memorable 1990/91 season had ended Harkes was a League Cup winner and instrumental in Wednesday earning immediate promotion back to the top flight. The versatile and highly likeable American remained a first team regular for a further two years before leaving for Derby County in August 1993, after 11 goals in 118 games for Wednesday. He is now a regular on ESPN's soccer coverage across the pond. When Ron Atkinson had originally taken Harkes on trial, he was joined at Hillsborough by compatriot, and former college team-mate, Tony Meola. The US international keeper played a solitary reserve game before the Owls decided not to follow up their initial interest. Along with Harkes, he appeared in the 1990 World Cup finals but returned to US domestic soccer after failing to make a breakthrough at either Brighton & Hove Albion or Watford. It was December 1993 before Trevor Francis invited US international forward Eric Wynalda for a week's trial. The all-time US top goalscorer had become the first US-born player to play professionally in Europe when he signed for German side Saarbrucken and after impressing in training at Wednesday he returned, in January 1994. However, Francis decided against bringing Wynalda to Sheffield on a permanent deal and he returned to the States, becoming the first-ever scorer in the MLS (Major League Soccer). The most recent addition was Frank Simek who signed in the summer of 2005. The St. Louis, Missouri-born right-back had joined Arsenal in 2002 but played only one League Cup tie for the London side, in addition to loan spells at QPR and AFC Bournemouth. After being signed by Paul Sturrock he became an automatic choice at right-back; his form resulting in several caps for the US in 2007. Unfortunately, a serious ankle injury – suffered at Crystal Palace in December 2007 - checked his Hillsborough progress and he was released in June 2010, signing for Carlisle United.

BAD TIMING

After winning promotion in 1980, Wednesday enjoyed a successful return to the second tier of the English game in the 1980/81 season, finishing in tenth place. The improvement continued as the Owls were subsequently one of the frontrunners for promotion throughout the following season. They found themselves in a great position, with just four games left to play, sitting in the third promotion spot. However, a rule change introduced in the previous summer – in an attempt to encourage attacking play – would scupper Jack Charlton's hopes of lifting Wednesday back into the top division for the first time since 1970. The decision by the Football League to introduce a new system of three points for a win was welcomed by clubs but Wednesday were one of the first 'victims' of the new rule. A defeat at Bolton Wanderers, in their final away game, ended any lingering promotion hopes and the final-day meeting with promotion-chasing Norwich City became academic. Wednesday won 2-1 on the day at Hillsborough against the Canaries, but it was the visitors who grabbed the last promotion spot – after Leicester City drew 0-0 with Shrewsbury Town – behind David Pleat's runaway champions Luton Town, and their close rivals Watford, who ended in the runners-up spot.

		P	W	D	L	F	A	Pts
1	Luton Town	42	25	13	4	86	46	88
2	Watford	42	23	11	8	76	42	80
3	Norwich City	42	22	5	15	64	50	71
4	WEDNESDAY	42	20	10	12	55	51	70

It was therefore left to Owls fans to mull over the fact that had the two-points-for-a-win rule lasted just one more season the final table would have had a very different look, and for supporters a return to the top flight would have been achieved, with trips to Old Trafford, Highbury and Anfield back on the agenda!

		P	W	D	L	F	A	Pts
1	Luton Town	42	25	13	4	86	46	63
2	Watford	42	23	11	8	76	42	57
3	WEDNESDAY	42	20	10	12	55	51	50
4	Norwich City	42	22	5	15	64	50	49

WHAT'S IN A NAME – 2

The area of Sheffield known as Hillsborough took its name from the Hillsborough Hall – the building where the library is now housed in Hillsborough Park. Built by the Steade family in 1779, the grand building was so named as a tribute to a family friend – Lord Downshire – who lived across the Irish Sea in Hillsborough, County Down. The area grew during the 19th century, from just a few cottages around Owlerton Green, and in 1901, two years after Wednesday moved into their new Owlerton home, the area of Hillsborough was incorporated into the City of Sheffield.

HAVEN'T WE FORGOTTEN SOMETHING?

Wednesday's preparations for their 1983 FA Cup semi-final against Brighton & Hove Albion did not get off to the best start as the team bus arrived at Arsenal's former home of Highbury missing two players! The departure time had been brought forward on police advice and it was not until the players were alighting at Highbury that it was noticed that both David Mills and Pat Heard had literally missed the bus. They did eventually catch up with their team-mates, looking rather sheepish no doubt!

ISLAND GIRL

Winger Michael Reddy scored five goals in 32 appearances for the Owls during two loan spells in 2003, memorably scoring last-minute winners against both Barnsley and champions-elect Portsmouth. He ended his playing days at League Two Grimsby Town and his career then took a rather unique path, which ended with Reddy playing amateur football for Falkland Islands-based club Port Stanley Albion! His route to the south Atlantic island began several thousand miles away when he moved to Greenland-based club Malamuk in 2007. It was while on the island that Reddy attended the Greenland Fishing Festival and met a girl from the Falkland Islands that soon became Mrs. Reddy. He duly emigrated to the small island, off the coast of Argentina, to live with his new bride and became the first student to take advantage of the FA's new 'remote teaching programme'. Lessons are delivered via an internet video link to his home in the Falkland Islands.

CAN WE PLAY YOU EVERY WEEK?

The 2008/09 season saw the Owls register a fourth consecutive double over Norwich City with only relegation from the Championship denying Wednesday the chance to stretch the record further.

2005/06	A	1-0	Brunt
	H	1-0	Tudgay
2006/07	A	2-1	Burton, Camp (og)
	H	3-2	Johnson, Burton, Etuhu (og)
2007/08	A	1-0	Small
	H	4-1	Burton 2, Sahar, Clarke
2008/09	H	3-2	McMahon, Clarke, Tudgay
	A	1-0	Johnson

MARDY BUM – 1

The October 2008 derby meeting with Sheffield United at Hillsborough proved to be somewhat controversial. What turned out to be the winning goal – scored by Steve Watson – put Wednesday ahead after Matt Kilgallon had been sent off, but after 69 minutes referee Mike Dean showed a second yellow card to Owls winger Jermaine Johnson. However, somewhat bizarrely, JJ had already been substituted and was on his way down the tunnel! After being replaced, the temperamental Jamaican showed his frustration by booting a water bottle into the crowd but his misdemeanour was spotted by the fourth official. JJ was given a second yellow card after being recalled from the dressing rooms. He therefore became the first Wednesday player to be sent off after already having left the field!

MIRACLE OF EWOOD PARK

Although watching Wednesday can bring both joy and pain, it should perhaps be added that it can also heal the sick. This was proven in the February 1993 League Cup semi-final at Blackburn Rovers when the Owls produced the finest 45 minutes of football by a Wednesday side in living memory. The Owls smashed four goals past Bobby Mimms at the roofless Darwen End terrace of Ewood Park and after each goal an Owls fan, stood behind the net, was seen to celebrate wildly by waving BOTH his crutches in the air!

THOSE WERE THE DAYS...

In the early days of organised football, it was fairly commonplace to see a Wednesday side consisting of several men wearing boots and trousers on the field of play. Often players dashed straight from work, didn't have time to change and therefore would think nothing of playing a match in their work clothes – to help identify which side was which, one side would tie a handkerchief to their arms to distinguish them from their opponents. Today's Health and Safety Executive would probably have had an opinion on the early footwear; to provide a better foothold those early pioneers did not think twice about hammering several nails into their boots... Thankfully, for players of that era the screw in stud was invented pretty soon after!

LEAGUE GAME # 1

After being voted into the Football League in 1892, Wednesday began a new era in their history with a trip to Notts County on Saturday 3rd September 1892. The close proximity of the first game prompted around 1,000 Wednesday fans to travel, swelling the gate at the Castle Ground to around 10,000. The ground was full to capacity and just before the teams took the field, the spectators broke down the barriers and flooded onto the pitch, causing the game to be delayed by 25 minutes. When the match eventually kicked off Wednesday were represented by the following eleven on that famous day:

> *William Allan, Tom Brandon, Albert Mumford, Sandy Hall, Billy Betts, Harry Brandon, Fred Spiksley, Alec Brady, Harry Davis, Sparrow Brown and Walter Dunlop.*

Wednesday dominated the early play and after 11 minutes a corner reached captain Tom Brandon and he fired the ball into the net to register the first goal Sheffield Wednesday scored in league football. At the interval two mounted policemen were brought into the ground to stop any further encroachment onto the pitch and it was Wednesday who held on to register a thoroughly deserved victory in a match that did not finish until half past five.

PAPERBACK WRITER

Ever been stuck for a really good book to read on holiday? Not sure what to buy a fellow Owl for Christmas? Since leaving Hillsborough, several players and managers have either written – or had biographies published – about their time at the club, and most with a few good tales from the Owls dressing room. These have ranged from books almost totally dominated by their Wednesday days to individuals who have spent only a relatively short time in Sheffield:

Viv ANDERSON	*First Among Unequals*
Len ASHURST	*Left Back in Time*
Ron ATKINSON	*A Different Ball Game*
Alan BROWN	*Coaching Man*
Lee CHAPMAN	*More Than a Match: A Player's Story*
Jack CHARLTON	*The Autobiography*
Jim CRAIG	*A Lion Looks Back*
Paolo DI CANIO	*The Autobiography*
Derek DOOLEY	*Dooley!*
John HARKES	*Captain For Life*
Brian MARWOOD	*Life of Brian*
Tommy TYNAN	*The Original Football Idol*
Jimmy SEED	*The Jimmy Seed Story*
Mel STERLAND	*Boozing, Betting & Brawling*
Peter SWAN	*Setting the Record Straight*
Chris WADDLE	*The Authorised Biography*
Billy WALKER	*Soccer in the Blood*
Howard WILKINSON	*Managing to Succeed*
Terry YORATH	*Hard Man, Hard Knocks*

In addition to those players who have told their story after leaving Wednesday, several had seen their stories told in print before they arrived at Hillsborough:

Graham COUGHLAN	*To be a Pilgrim*
Trevor FRANCIS	*Anatomy of a £1m Player*
Willie HENDERSON	*Forward with Rangers*
Paul STURROCK	*Forward Thinking*

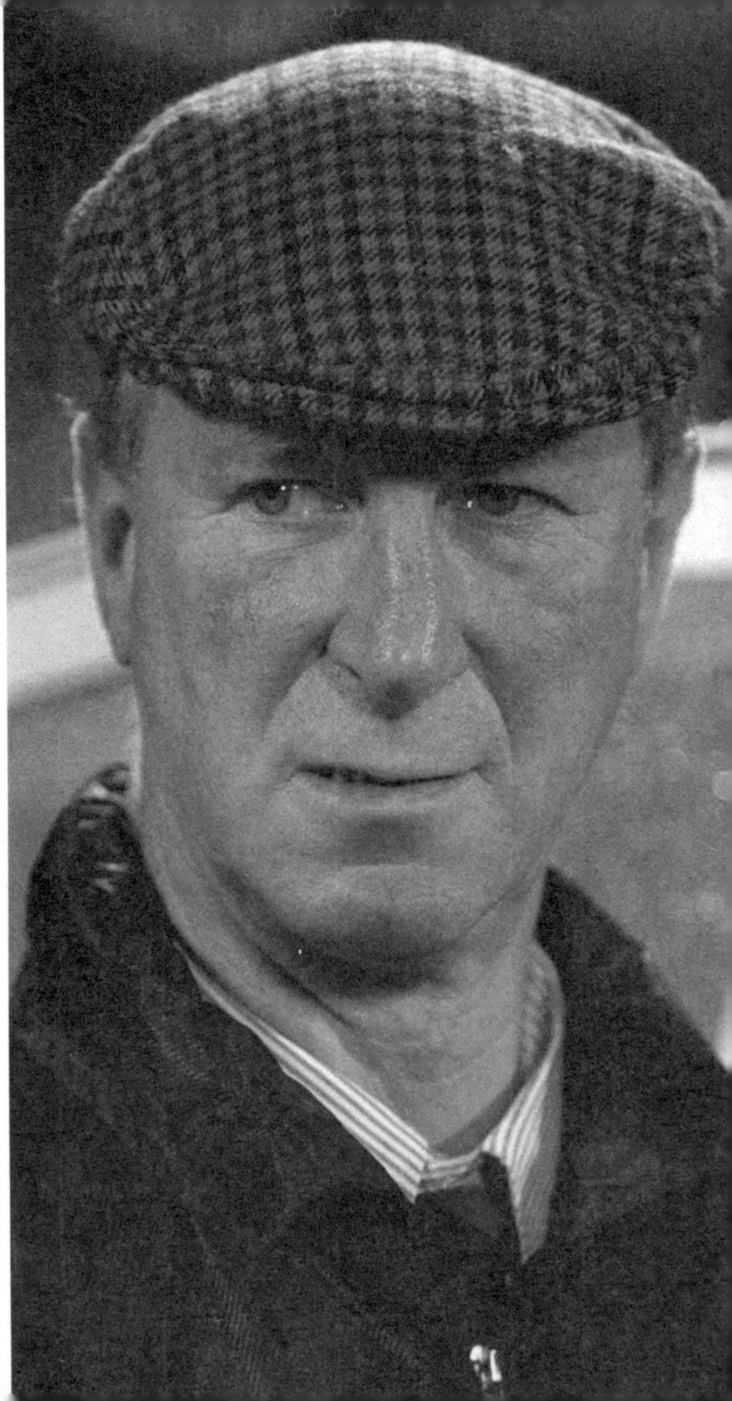

JACK CHARLTON – WEDNESDAY MANAGER 1977-83

GREAT ESCAPE – 2

After reclaiming their First Division place in 1926, Wednesday finished just below mid-table in their first season back in the big time. However, they then experienced a terrible start to the 1927/28 season, winning only one of their first 12 games. Unfortunately, Wednesday's fortunes failed to improve and with just ten games left they seemed doomed to relegation after tasting victory in just six league games.

Bottom of Division One – 17/03/1928

		P	W	D	L	F	A	Pts
14	Liverpool	33	11	9	13	73	69	31
15	Birmingham City	33	9	13	11	55	62	31
16	Derby County	32	11	8	13	72	72	30
17	Aston Villa	31	12	6	13	62	62	30
18	Middlesbrough	33	10	10	13	69	71	30
19	Manchester United	32	11	7	14	49	56	29
20	Sheffield United	32	11	7	14	59	68	29
21	Portsmouth	32	11	7	14	51	73	29
22	WEDNESDAY	32	6	10	16	56	67	22

Despite beating Liverpool 4-0 in their next match, the situation still looked hopeless. Incredibly, Wednesday, inspired by former Tottenham player Jimmy Seed, then secured a 2-2 draw at high-flying Leicester City before a brace from Mark Hooper and a strike from Jimmy Seed took the Owls to a 3-1 Good Friday win at Spurs. A string of four consecutive wins in April 1928 suddenly made Owls fans believe that an incredible escape from the drop could actually become reality. A last-minute goal from Jimmy Seed, in the final away game of the season at Arsenal, lifted Wednesday off the bottom of the division, and out of the two relegation places, for the first time since December 1927. Amazingly, the bottom four teams all had 37 points to their name with just one game to play while only two points separated 12th-place Liverpool from bottom club Manchester United! The final day was set for the greatest relegation dogfight of all time and an expectant crowd of 36,636 were inside Hillsborough to see if the Owls could complete the remarkable Houdini act by beating visitors Aston Villa. The game was tied 0-0 at the break but two minutes into the second period Jack Allen fired home from Mark Hooper's cross and the ground erupted. The win was secured with 15 minutes left when the visiting goalie totally missed a cross, allowing Jimmy Trotter to tap the ball into the empty net and seal the club's First Division status. The full-time whistle sparked wild scenes of celebration after Wednesday had registered an eighth win from their final 12 matches. The bottom two clubs at 3.00pm on that final Saturday – Manchester United and Sunderland – both saved their bacon and it was Middlesbrough who took the drop along with a Spurs side who were on their way to a friendly in Holland, never imagining that their First Division safety was in danger! Spurs' demise was an irony not lost on Wednesday captain Seed, as he had been deemed surplus to requirements at White Hart Lane but had returned to haunt his old club and help in their surprise relegation.

Division One – Final Table – 1927/28

		P	W	D	L	F	A	Pts
14	WEDNESDAY	42	13	13	16	81	78	39
15	Sunderland	42	15	9	18	74	76	39
16	Liverpool	42	13	13	16	84	87	39
17	West Ham	42	14	11	17	81	88	39
18	Manchester United	42	16	7	19	72	80	39
19	Burnley	42	16	7	19	82	98	39
20	Portsmouth	42	16	7	19	66	90	39
21	Tottenham	42	15	8	19	74	86	38
22	Middlesbrough	42	11	15	16	81	88	37

THE GOALKEEPER'S SCORED!

Despite the modern tactic of sending the goalie up for set pieces in the dying seconds, the chance of seeing a goalkeeper score from open play is still extremely rare. However, Wednesday fans have been fortunate to see this feat achieved twice at Hillsborough in the last 25 years. The first man was Coventry City custodian Steve Ogrizovic who scored after 62 minutes of a 2-2 draw on October 25th 1986. The keeper had cleared the ball upfield and was stunned when it promptly landed and bounced straight over Wednesday keeper Martin Hodge and into the net! The only instance of a Wednesday keeper scoring in a senior game came as recently as December 23rd 2006 when Mark Crossley was waved up for Chris Brunt's 93rd-minute corner and duly headed home to make the score 3-3 and send Hillsborough into raptures!

SACK THE KIT DESIGNER!

Owls officials were rather red faced in September 1993 when Wednesday travelled to Newcastle United for a live Sky TV game. It was obvious that the club's striped kit would clash with the home team's black and white so instead Wednesday packed a new, hastily manufactured, third kit of black and white! The all white shirt, with black pin stripes was therefore merged with yellow shorts for a rather fetching ensemble. The colour clash did not however faze the Geordies who won 4-2 to extend the Owls' winless start to the new season.

MANY HAPPY RETURNS

Celebrations of the Owls' 100th birthday – in September 1967 – could not have started better as a goal from John Ritchie secured a 1-0 win at Bramall Lane in a top-flight game. Four days later Wednesday designated the home game with Fulham as a celebration match, cutting ticket prices in half and presenting every supporter with a centenary pin badge as they came through the turnstiles. The team also marked the special occasion by recording a 4-2 win which, rather fittingly, left Wednesday top of the First Division table. Ironically, the birthday was actually celebrated a day late as back in 1967 it was still believed that the club had been formed on September 5th, when it was actually the 4th!

WIN BONUS

In the early years of Wednesday's history it was common practice for the winning side to share a gallon of beer after a game, while the losers had to make do with just half! This post-match ritual eventually died out as Wednesday turned pro.

MASS CLEAR OUT

Wednesday manager Chris Turner made headlines in the summer of 2004 when he released 13 players after the Owls had finished 16th in today's League One; the club's second-worst final position of all time. The likes of Alan Quinn and Kevin Pressman were shown the door but this cull of the playing staff seemed positively restrained when compared with the summer of 1920 when, following relegation from the First Division, the club released or transferred a mere 21 players!

BACK FROM THE DEAD

Until recently, all the evidence available suggested that pre-World War I player James Monaghan had been one of the estimated 20 million people killed in the bloodiest war in human history. The fact that Wednesday's own minute book stated they had held a collection for Monaghan's family in 1918 seemingly confirmed the sad tale that James had indeed been lost in the conflict. However, in November 2008 a posting on fans' website 'Owlstalk' set in motion a chain of events that confirmed the fact that James Monaghan had died on the frontline. Incredibly, though, it was not the same James Monaghan that had appeared twice for Wednesday in December 1913 but a man of the same name, from the same area, serving in the same regiment! In September 1916, he suffered temporary blindness during the second bloody battle of the Somme when a bullet penetrated his temple and exited through his eye. The story is no better told than in the words of James Monaghan himself who recalled that he was left for dead in no-man's-land, delirious in a shell hole, and was only rescued when he was heard shouting. He was rescued and taken to the Durham Light Infantry dressing station, a fact that it's believed led to his death being incorrectly reported as his regiment assumed that he had died on the battlefield. Unbelievably, on the same day, the 'other' James Monaghan was fatally injured and this story of mistaken identity led to the Ministry of Defence giving the wrong news to both sets of families. His family even went to the local Co-op to get their black mourning clothes before the incredible error came to light. It also transpired that the two James Monaghans had an agreement that if either one was killed the family of the survivor should pay condolences to the other – his sister still remembers a stranger coming to the house after Jim's death was reported, presumably from the other Monaghan's family... After his rescue, Jim was taken back to London for surgery, being discharged from hospital in April 1917. He returned home and after the war worked as a telephonist, having been trained by St. Dunstan's, a charity set up after the conflict for blind and visually impaired soldiers. He later worked in a bank while incredibly, for a man who was supposed to be dead, he lived a long life, dying at the grand old age of 96 in Newcastle on December 22nd 1989.

EVERYBODY PILE ON!

In January 1914, Wednesday beat Notts County 3-2 at Hillsborough in an FA Cup first round tie. However, the game was not without controversy, with the winning goal for the Owls fiercely contested by the Nottingham side. The incident in question occurred in the second half when, from a corner, the ball was grabbed by County goalie Albert Iremonger. Within seconds he was covered in a mass of blue and white shirts with the referee struggling to keep trace of the ball! The whistle then sounded and most fans in the ground expected the away side to be awarded a free kick for the fairly obvious foul on the visiting custodian. This was not the case, though, as the referee ran towards the halfway line having awarded a goal to Wednesday! Poor old Iremonger, with the ball still in his grasp, was helped to his feet before collapsing and being carried unconscious into the dressing room. It would be fair to say the concussed goalie was extremely unfortunate as County reported that when he had initially received the ball from the flag kick he was kicked several times in the head during the ensuing scramble and that the ball was not even over the line. It was a man's game in those days!

ELEMENTARY MY DEAR WATSON

Former Everton and Newcastle player Steve Watson may have only netted six times in 59 appearances for Sheffield Wednesday but when he scored, it did tend to be pretty crucial. His most famous moment in an Owls shirt was the winning goal against Sheffield United at Hillsborough in October 2008, which set the Owls on their way to a subsequent double over steel city rivals the Blades. His first goal for Wednesday was scored deep into stoppage time to grab a 1-1 draw at high-flying West Bromwich Albion in November 2007. He scored twice more during that season; putting the Owls ahead in the 1-1 FA Cup draw at home to Derby County and, crucially, scoring the second goal of the hugely important 3-1 relegation win at Leicester City in April 2008. His two other goals in a Wednesday shirt also secured a point – 1-1 draws at Swansea City and Ipswich Town – and he proved a somewhat lucky omen before being forced to retire from the game due to injury in the summer of 2009.

FORTRESS HILLSBOROUGH

After moving to their new Owlerton ground in 1899, Wednesday were virtually unbeatable there for 14 months. They posted a 100% Second Division home record in their first season at their new home. After beating Chesterfield 5-1 in the opening match of the campaign, the club proceeded to win the remaining sixteen games, scoring a staggering 61 times and a miserly defence only conceded seven goals. Unsurprisingly, this is the only occasion in Wednesday's history that this unique feat has been achieved, and the sequence was actually stretched to 19 games before Preston North End became the first visiting team to beat the club at Hillsborough, winning 1-0 in October 1900.

I'VE STARTED SO I'LL (NOT) FINISH

The club's first abandoned game was way back in 1871 and for a reason unlikely to cause an abandonment in the current day. The game was called off when neither Wednesday, nor their opponents the MacKenzie Club, could produce another ball after the original burst! In pre-league football Wednesday were awarded a cup tie when eight of their opponents' players walked off the pitch in protest at a goal scored by Wednesday. During the First World War, a match was abandoned when a football game broke out in the middle of a boxing match involving the players and half the crowd! In competitive peacetime football, the following games involving Wednesday have failed to reach their conclusion:

18/11/1893	Stoke FC	Division 1 (h) 0-0	Snow
25/11/1893	Darwen	Division 1 (a) 0-1	Rain
30/12/1893	Darwen	Division 1 (h) 2-2	Fog
06/04/1895	Stoke FC	Division 1 (h) 0-0	Crowd disorder
26/11/1898	Aston Villa	Division 1 (h) 3-1	Poor light
10/02/1900	Sheffield U	FA Cup (a) 0-0	Snow
22/02/1936	Birmingham	Division 1 (a) 0-1	Snow
19/11/1949	Coventry C	Division 2 (a) 0-1	Fog
09/12/1967	Arsenal	Division 1 (a) 0-1	Snow
20/01/1973	Bristol City	Division 2 (h) 0-0	Snow
01/11/1975	Walsall	Division 3 (a) 0-0	Rain
08/12/2007	Coventry C	Championship (h) 0-0	Rain

GOAL AVERAGE TO THE RESCUE

In the final season (1938/39) before World War II broke out in September 1939, Wednesday were beaten to promotion from the Second Division by a single point by city rivals United. Eleven years later the Sheffield sides were again fighting for one of the two promotion places from the second tier. With five games remaining, Wednesday were second to Tottenham but then lost 1-0 on the south coast at Southampton – a result that put the Saints into the promotion shake up – before being held 1-1 at home to Coventry City. Four days later the Owls were back on course when a Walter Rickett hat-trick helped to beat Grimsby Town 4-0 at Hillsborough. The fight for promotion took another twist in the club's final away game of the season as West Ham United scored twice in the first half to leave Wednesday with a mountain to climb. However, Eric Taylor's side were not to be beaten and goals early in the second half at Upton Park, from Dennis Woodhead and Redfern Froggatt, meant they rescued a point and ensured that three clubs – Wednesday, United and Southampton – were still in with a chance with just one game remaining. Luckily for Wednesday, their city rivals finished their season early – beating Hull City 5-0 at Bramall Lane to jump into the second promotion spot. This meant it was a two-horse race between Wednesday and Southampton to leapfrog United and reach the top flight. The use of goal average (goals scored/goals conceded) meant that there was a myriad of possibilities but Wednesday knew that a 0-0 draw, in their home game with champions Spurs, would be enough to clinch promotion. In front of a very nervous 50,853 Hillsborough crowd, the game swung from end to end but despite a few scares the Owls secured the result they needed which meant they were back in the First Division after an absence of 13 years.

Division Two

	P	W	D	L	F	A	Pts
Tottenham Hotspur	42	27	7	8	81	35	61
Sheffield Wednesday	42	18	16	8	67	48	52
Sheffield United	42	19	14	9	68	49	52
Southampton	42	19	14	9	64	48	52
Leeds United	42	17	13	12	54	45	47

HERE'S THE FOG YOU ORDERED, MR PLEAT!

Losing players to – often meaningless – international fixtures is never particularly welcomed by any club manager but 1990s Wednesday boss David Pleat could well have used a higher power to get around the inconvenience in March 1997. The Owls were due to play Sunderland in a Premiership game at Hillsborough but were set to be without the services of Yugoslavian Dejan Stefanovic, who was scheduled to fly from Heathrow Airport to report for national duty. However, somewhat luckily for Wednesday, fog duly descended upon the London airport, causing all outgoing flights to be cancelled. This unforeseen development allowed Stefanovic to return to Sheffield where he subsequently crashed home the winning goal as Sunderland were beaten 2-1!

FA CUP DEBUT

Wednesday made their debut in the world's oldest and most famous cup competition back in 1880, and were drawn at leading Scottish side Queen's Park in the first round. However, the game never took place as the famous amateur club conceded the tie – allowing their opponents a walkover into the second round. The Owls' first actual game in the cup was therefore at renowned cup fighters Blackburn Rovers with the new boys rated as underdogs. It was a decision on footwear that would effectively settle the game as due to an icy pitch Wednesday adopted a kind of leather stud while Rovers fitted strips of felt to the soles of their boots. Most of the 2,000 crowd thought the Yorkshire visitors had made the wrong choice but it was Blackburn who could not keep their feet and Wednesday 'skated' to a 4-0 win with forward Bob Gregory scoring three of the second-half goals. Three weeks later Wednesday travelled to Lancashire for a second time, to face a club called Turton, where goals from Gregory and Rhodes sent them into a fourth round that, rather confusingly, contained twelve teams! The upstarts from Sheffield had certainly made headlines in their first season in the competition but their run came to an end as Darwen won 5-2 – as Wednesday were drawn away for the fourth time – in February 1881. Incidentally the Owls' conquerors beat Romford 15-0 in the next round before losing 4-1 to Old Carthusians in the semi-final; eventual runners-up Old Etonians received a bye in the semi-finals!

I PREDICT A RIOT

After making a good start to the 1980/81 season, after gaining promotion from the Third Division under Jack Charlton, Wednesday made the short trip to Oldham Athletic standing in third place in the fledgling league table. However, it would be off the field events that would grab the headlines and put the club and its so-called fans in the FA dock. Future Owl (and former Blade) Simon Stainrod opened the scoring after ten minutes but it was his clash with Wednesday favourite Terry Curran after 26 minutes that led to ugly scenes on the terraces. The duo had initially clashed but as the referee was booking both players Curran appeared to kick out at his rival, who subsequently fell to the ground in a somewhat theatrical manner. The official instantly sent off Curran and at this point a minor riot broke out on the away end with Owls fans incensed that their folk hero had been so controversially sent off. The crowd disturbance lasted for a full 27 minutes before Wednesday staff managed to calm the situation down and the game could be played to a conclusion. Oldham scored again in the final minute to complete a 2-0 win. Nine days after the game, Wednesday were called before an FA commission and were hit heavily with fines and sanctions:

1 All standing areas to be closed at Hillsborough for the next four home games.
2 The next four away games to be made all-ticket with no sales to Wednesday fans.
3 Wednesday to pay their away opponents compensation of £3,000 each for loss of revenue from away ticket sales.

In addition, the Owls imposed two-season Hillsborough bans on any fans found guilty of any charge committed inside Boundary Park on that fateful day. All ground season ticket holders at Hillsborough were subsequently housed in the uncovered seats at the front of the South Stand while any casual fan had no choice but to pay the higher price for a seat if he wanted to see the Owls play – a small financial uplift for the club, which the FA had probably not intended! As for the away ban, this was seen as a challenge by the majority of the travelling army and when Wednesday scored at Swansea in the first 'away ban' game the cheers from the terraces suggested more than a handful of travelling fans had somehow found the way into the Vetch Field. Owls captain Mike Lyons commented; "They'll get where water won't."

QUOTES FROM THE PAST - 1

"There is no doubt that we owe a very great deal to the splendid support we have received from you this season. I can hardly speak; I am almost overcome by the splendid fight our chaps have made. Believe me, your vocal support had a lot to do with us getting the equaliser today. Your help was a telling factor last season; but I do not think you have ever made a bigger effort for us than just before we got our equalising goal"

Wednesday captain, Jimmy Seed, talking to the Hillsborough crowd after a 1-1 draw with Burnley had clinched the title in April 1929

"I just told Shez to get out of the way. I've been waiting to do that all season"

Chris Waddle on his first-minute Wembley goal against the Blades in April 1993

"I have been hunting for this cup for 20 years"

Wednesday president John Holmes after the 1896 FA Cup Final victory over Wolves

"We shall definitely not be playing for a draw; that would be courting trouble. The attitude of the players is right and they feel confident"

Manager Len Ashurst before Wednesday beat Southend United in April 1976 to stave off relegation to the bottom division

DJ SUPERSTAR

A familiar voice on the Hillsborough scene in the 1980s was DJ Steve Splash – real name Steve Evans. He became the club's matchday disc jockey in 1980 and for several years ran his own mobile DJ business, supplying DJs for various functions around the city. Before moving back to Sheffield, Steve had worked for a time in Spain and, after being convinced by friends, he attended a trial at Real Racing de Santander and played several games for the Spanish club's reserve side. During his time at the club the senior side gained promotion to the top division in Spain but a knee injury ruined any chances he had of challenging for a first team place. The end of his playing career, his poor Spanish and homesickness eventually saw Steve return home to Yorkshire.

BACK IN THE USSR

At the end of the 1959/60 season, Wednesday embarked on an ambitious close-season tour of what was then known as the Union of Soviet Socialist Republics (USSR). This huge area encompassed fifteen 'union republics' of which many are now independent states in modern-day Europe, such as Latvia, Armenia and Moldova. Wednesday commenced their tour in the Russian capital of Moscow where in front of a 50,000-strong crowd, in the Central Lenin Stadium, they lost 1-0 to Soviet Army side CSKA Moscow. The Owls then travelled over 1,000 miles south to Tiflis – in Georgia – where Ron Springett saved a first-half penalty as Wednesday went in at the interval 0-0 with hosts Tbilisi Dynamo. A highly controversial penalty – after John Martin had made a seemingly perfect tackle in the area – scored by Meschi after 74 minutes won the game for the Georgians. The Owls' travel itinerary then meant it was all the way back to the Central Lenin Stadium, Moscow where they met Locomotiv Moscow on June 1st 1960! The Muscovites raced into a 3-0 lead early in the second half but a brace from Alan Finney meant the Westerners went home with pride intact after three narrow defeats behind the 'Iron Curtain'. In November 1960, Tbilisi made a reciprocal visit to Sheffield but on home turf the Owls were masters, winning 5-0 in front of 38,778 fans, with John Fantham scoring four times.

FROZEN NORTH (AND SOUTH, EAST AND WEST)

The winters of 1946 and 1962 were without doubt the worst experienced in English football with the Owls amazingly finishing the 1946/47 season on the first Saturday of June! The club had suffered a catalogue of postponements during the first three months of that year and in those pre-floodlight days, they were limited in the re-arrangement of fixtures. The final home game of the season was played on May 26th before a 12-day gap preceded the aforementioned finale at Saltergate. The winter of 1962/63 was arguably even worse as between December 30th 1962 and March 1st 1963 Wednesday played only once – an FA Cup draw at Shrewsbury Town. When the big thaw finally started in March, the club was faced with a mountain of fixtures to cram into the final weeks of the season – playing thirteen league games in just 46 days.

FRENCH FARCE – 1

A total of 78 goals in 187 appearances plainly reflected the value of centre forward Lee Chapman to the Owls in the 1980s. After being rescued by Wednesday boss Howard Wilkinson, after nightmare spells at Arsenal and then Sunderland, he fitted perfectly into the Owls' high tempo game and became an instant hit with Hillsborough fans; he was voted Player of the Year in 1987. It was therefore a surprise when Chapman refused a new deal from the Owls in the summer of 1988 and looked set for a highly lucrative move to Greek side PAOK Salonika. That deal, however, collapsed and instead he moved to obscure French Division Two (South) club Niort. With the two sides unable to agree a fee, Wednesday had no choice but to leave the matter in the hands of a Uefa transfer committee – the Owls asking £350,000 for the Lincoln-born attacker, while Niort offered just £193,000. Whilst this was all occurring, Chapman had moved to France, was taking language lessons, and generally adapting to life in a foreign country. As the saga rumbled on, Chapman was unable to play and his days in French soccer looked set to end prematurely when the tribunal set a fee of £290,000 and Niort admitted they could not afford to pay the price! A frustrated Howard Wilkinson commented: "It does seem Niort cannot meet their obligations. They are being asked for £100,000 more than they want to pay and as a result they have decided, presumably, that they cannot fulfil their end of the agreement. What it means is that Sheffield Wednesday have, at this moment, neither the money or the player." At this point it seemed likely that Chapman would return to Sheffield but the French side hit upon a better idea – they sold Chapman back to an English club for a tidy £60,000 profit; Nottingham Forest effectively paying the Owls for Chapman and giving Niort a finder's fee!

TRAINSPOTTING – 2

Exactly 50 years after a steam locomotive bearing the club's name was decommissioned, the Owls were honoured again when a loco was named in their honour. The official ceremony took place at Sheffield railway station on September 11th 2009 with Wednesday becoming only the second club in the county, after Sunderland, to have their name emblazoned on a serving loco.

THE (NOT SO) SECRET GAME

The first match to be played under floodlights at Hillsborough was Derek Dooley's benefit game in March 1955 but it would be seven months before Wednesday would play a competitive evening game. Their opponents, in a County Cup tie, would be neighbours United but a month before the game the Owls invited the Blades to take part in a closed-doors friendly to help the players adapt to the 'alien' experience of playing under generated light. Wednesday also wanted to experience floodlight football as crack Hungarian side Vasas Budapest were due at Hillsborough for a glamour friendly five days later. Only 30 spectators were allowed into the ground including the managers, directors and two pressmen, who were only granted admittance if they vowed not to disclose any details of the game. As the match was being played, a police car patrolled around the ground with one intrepid fan being ordered off the stand roof as he tried to get a glimpse of the action! Supporters who were queuing for tickets for the aforementioned Vasas game were bluntly told "Sorry, it's a private trial" when requesting a score check. The following day's *Sheffield Morning Telegraph* reported on how impressive the new floodlights were but kept their promise of not revealing the result although the reporter did admit it was a "shock score". The Owls secretary-manager Eric Taylor commented; "I am satisfied that the match was worthwhile. It proved valuable match practice and we may repeat the experience." Unfortunately, the Owls' good intentions of keeping the score quiet were blown out of the water as the *News Chronicle* paper duly printed a full report of the game, including line-ups, which revealed Wednesday had thrashed their neighbours 7-2! After the report appeared, Taylor described the act as a "shabby trick" and no doubt scrapped any ideas of repeating the exercise. The irony was probably not lost on Wednesday fans when United won the 'proper game' 5-2 on November 2nd 1955!

| WEDNESDAY | 7 | Sewell 3, Shiner 3, Quixall |
| UNITED | 2 | Ringstead, Wragg (pen) |

Wednesday: McIntosh, Staniforth, Bingley, Gibson, McEvoy, Kay (T. McAnearney ht), Froggatt, Sewell, Shiner, Quixall, Broadbent

United: Thompson, Coldwell, Mason, Hoyland, Shaw, Iley, Ringstead, Howitt, Wragg, Rawson, Grainger

MAN FLU

Plans for the 1957/58 season slowly started to unravel the moment player Jack Shaw reported sick with influenza. Within days the club was hit by a flu epidemic that decimated the playing and coaching staff. Five days before Wednesday's opening day game at Manchester City a total of seven players were affected and 48 hours later the Football League agreed to postpone the first game of the new campaign – the first time this had happened in English football. The story made national headlines and the club's away game at Newcastle United was also called off before the season eventually started – seven days late – with the visit of Nottingham Forest to Hillsborough. Defender Norman Curtis was worst affected by the outbreak – he was close to pneumonia – while the season as a whole proved somewhat of a disaster as Wednesday were relegated from the top flight for the third time in the decade.

FARM BOY

Brought up in the Kent coastal resort of Deal, future Wednesday goalkeeper Bob Bolder lived just a hundred yards from the town's pebble beach and spent endless hours there as a child sunbathing, swimming and picnicking. Whilst at secondary school his work experience sent him to a local farm where he cut and packed vegetables. At the age of 15, he attended trials at Charlton Athletic but Bolder was short, and somewhat scrawny, for his age and this meant he returned home with hopes of a professional career dashed. After leaving school, he returned to life on the farm and, for two and a half years, worked in the open air, cultivating, ploughing and labouring. The hard work totally changed his physical appearance as Bolder shot up to 6ft 3in in height, and to almost 14st in weight. By this time, he was playing regularly for Dover Athletic in the Southern League and it was to the Kent side that Wednesday paid £1,000 in March 1977 to obtain his services. He proved to be a bargain buy, as he amassed 224 games for the club prior to moving to Liverpool in 1983 for a £125,000 fee. His career turned full circle in 1986 when he signed for the club who'd rejected him as a youngster, Charlton Athletic. He spent eight years at the London club and in April 1995 Wednesday played out a 3-3 draw at the Valley in a benefit game for the goalie.

FOR THE BENEFIT OF

The increasingly transient nature of the modern game has meant that testimonial and benefit games are slowly disappearing from the football calendar. In times past a player's benefit year would arguably be the biggest money spinner in his career, particularly in the days of the maximum wage, and was seen by fans as a fitting reward for a player's loyal service to a club (a testimonial would usually be granted for ten years' service). In other instances, a benefit would be awarded for reasons of injury, the tragic case of Derek Dooley being an extreme example. Since the war, the following Wednesday boys have been honoured:

Derek Dooley 1955 .... Sheffield XI 1-5 International XI
Doug McMillan 1961 .... Sheffield XI 5-8 Select XI
Redfern Froggatt 1962 .... Wednesday 2-2 Ajax Amsterdam
Derek Wilkinson 1966 .... Wednesday 8-7 All Stars
Ron Springett 1967 .... Wednesday 3-2 Sheffield United
Don Megson 1969 .... Wednesday 7-7 International XI
Gerry Young 1970 .... Wednesday 3-3 Sheffield United
John Fantham 1970 .... Sheffield XI 4-8 John Fantham XI
Eric Taylor 1974 .... Wednesday 0-5 England XI
Neil O'Donnell 1977 .... Wednesday 2-0 Norwich City
Mick Prendergast 1977 .... Wednesday 2-3 Leicester City
Paul Bradshaw 1979 .... Wednesday 4-2 Leeds United
Jimmy Mullen 1980 .... Wednesday 3-1 Manchester City
Mark Smith 1986 .... Wednesday 3-1 Sheffield United
Lawrie Madden 1990 .... Wednesday 3-0 Sheffield United
Nigel Worthington 1993 .... Wednesday 1-1 Derby County
David Hirst 2000 .... Owls '93 8-4 Premier League All Stars

HENDERSON'S RELISH

Signed in the summer of 1972 from Glasgow Rangers, popular winger Willie Henderson was famously so short sighted that he only crossed the ball when he actually set eyes on the touchline chalk. During his days with Rangers, he once took a seat on the Celtic bench, blissfully unaware of the somewhat hostile stares of the men in green and white!

PENALTY KINGS

Although it seems almost impossible to miss from 12 yards, the number of penalties spurned every week proves that this is simply not the case. Over the years, the Owls have boasted several players who were excellent from the spot but two men take the plaudits as the penalty kings. Wednesday finished the 1932/33 season in third place in the First Division and were helped by the awarding of 14 penalties in their favour. Centre forward Jack Ball was handed the ball on every occasion, scoring ten from 14:

> Scored: v Blackpool (h), Blackburn Rovers (h), Wolves (a), Huddersfield Town (h), Aston Villa (a), Middlesbrough (h), Manchester City (h), Arsenal (h), Leeds United (h – 2 goals)

> Missed: v Newcastle United (h), Bolton Wanderers (a), Manchester City (h), Wolves (h)

It seemed highly unlikely that this mark would ever be bettered but in the 1979/80 promotion season Wednesday were awarded a total of 15 penalties. On this occasion, the spot kicks were shared between three different players with Brian Hornsby and Jeff King missing one each. The rest were left to Mark Smith whose successful kick against Gillingham on April 7th 1980 bettered Ball's long-standing record:

> Scored: v Manchester City (FLC) (a), Millwall (a), Swindon Town (h), Chesterfield (a), Wimbledon (a), Lincoln City (FAC) (h), Sheffield United (h), Colchester United (h – 2 goals), Bury (h), Gillingham (h)

> Missed: v Chesterfield (h), Exeter City (a)

GREAT START

The 14-game unbeaten start to the 1899/00 season stood as the Owls' best start to a league campaign for over 80 years, before being bettered by Howard Wilkinson's 1983/84 team. A Mike Lyons goal on the opening day of the season gave Wednesday the perfect start and it would not be until the 16th Second Division game of the season that defeat was suffered for the first time – losing 1-0 at Crystal Palace on November 26th 1983.

Aug 27	Swansea City (a) 1-0	Lyons
Aug 29	Derby County (a) 1-1	Bannister
Sep 03	Carlisle United (h) 2-0	Bannister, O'Riordan (og)
Sep 06	Cambridge United (h) 1-0	Varadi
Sep 10	Charlton Athletic (a) 1-1	Dowman (og)
Sep 17	Chelsea (h) 2-1	Lyons, Megson
Sep 24	Oldham Athletic (a) 3-1	Varadi, Shelton, Sterland
Oct 01	Blackburn Rovers (h) 4-2	Sterland, Lyons, Bannister, Varadi
Oct 08	Leeds United (h) 3-1	Shelton, Pearson, Morris
Oct 15	Portsmouth (a) 1-0	Megson
Oct 22	Brighton & HA (a) 3-1	Pearson, Madden, Bannister
Oct 29	Huddersfield Town (h) 0-0	
Nov 05	Barnsley (h) 2-0	Smith, Sterland
Nov 11	Fulham (a) 1-1	Cunningham
Nov 19	Newcastle United (h) 4-2	Varadi 2, Cunningham, Bannister

THE SHOCK OF THE LIGHTNING

Born in Heeley in 1884, Walter Holbem graduated from local football to appear in 89 senior games for Wednesday between 1905 and 1911. After making his name at left-back during his spell at Owlerton, he moved to Everton for what was a fairly large fee in those days of £500 and ended his playing days at Southport Central, before settling in the area. After hanging up his boots, Holbem stayed in sport and became a bookmaker – but it was this profession that led directly to his tragic death in June 1930 at Ascot races. During the second race of the day, a huge crack of thunder was heard above the course and as the horses in the Royal Hunt Cup crossed the finish line the heavens opened with torrential rain, thunder and lightning striking the course. It was during this deluge that Holbem's metal framed umbrella was hit directly by a bolt of lightning, ripping the umbrella to pieces and striking poor old Walter in the throat. He fell to the ground, unconscious instantly. Sadly he would never recover from the strike, and he died in hospital later that day.

QUOTES FROM THE PAST – 2

"I am proud of my team. They showed what they can do, and I'll tell you this – they will be back again. Nothing will stop that. They're young lads mostly, five under 21 and one just 21. They could be playing for Wednesday again in the next six or seven cup finals, and probably more than that. I am disappointed for them today. They tried… how they tried. I'm the proudest man in the world because of them. After all, defeat doesn't mean everything. If you have to be beaten in the cup what better time than the final. Getting to Wembley was their big achievement."

Wednesday manager, Alan Brown, in bullish mood after a 3-2 defeat to Everton in the 1966 FA Cup Final.

"I've played at Wembley, but I was looking forward to this more. I never got nervous, just excited, I'm now happy, really happy."

Terry Curran after the Boxing Day 1979 win over Sheffield United

"The grave news is that Derek Dooley has had his right leg amputated above the knee."

The hospital statement that stunned the football world in February 1953.

"This was better than winning the Uefa Cup with Gothenburg, with the atmosphere and the crowd. They were incredible. I'm walking on air, it's just fantastic"

Roland Nilsson after the 1991 League Cup final win over Manchester United.

"It has been an honour to captain this club and to win promotion and lift a trophy at the Millennium Stadium is the biggest thing I will ever do in my career."

Owls captain Lee Bullen after the 2005 League One play-off win.

"Are you the Greaves who gets all the goals?"

Ron Springett's polite question to Jimmy Greaves after the Spurs attacker had again failed to score past him.

"Winning promotion is like having a prison sentence quashed"

Ron Atkinson in May 1991 after Bristol City were beaten to win promotion.

"Exeter were the only team to do the double over us in the league, that's not bad; and I'll settle for that and promotion; and the fans – they were terrific."

Manager Jack Charlton on promotion in 1980

HEALTH RISK

Watching the Owls can certainly be a highly stressful pastime – especially when they are attempting to defend a lead – but no-one has suffered like attacker Charlie Binney. In May 1923, he reported sick after suffering a nervous breakdown. Thankfully, he recovered, after spending time away from the smoke of Sheffield, but his illness marked the end of Binney's professional career, re-starting his football career with Worksop Town in 1925.

HE NEVER MISSES

Inter-war wing wizard Mark Hooper set a new club record, appearing in 189 consecutive games over a four-year period. He started his amazing run in a 3-1 win at Tottenham on April 6th 1928, playing the final eight First Division games of the season, with the run ending in April 1932 when he missed the final away match of the season at Manchester City. His run in the side coincided with back-to-back title successes in 1929 and 1930.

Season	League	Cup	Total
1927/28	8	0	8
1928/29	42	2	52
1929/30	42	6	100
1930/31	42	2	144
1931/32	40	5	189

It was over 50 years before the record was bettered by keeper Martin Hodge; he amassed 214 consecutive games: from his debut at Swansea City on August 27th 1983 until injury ended the run at Southampton in October 1987. He arrived as supposed understudy to England under-21 keeper Iain Hesford. But, it was Hodge who got the nod from Howard Wilkinson for the opening game of the season. Hesford never played a senior game for the club!

Season	League	Cup	Total
1983/84	42	11	53
1984/85	42	10	105
1985/86	42	10	157
1986/87	42	10	209
1987/88	5	0	214

FOOTBALL ALLIANCE LEAGUE

After failing to gain election into the Football League in the summer of 1889, Wednesday took direct action by becoming a driving force in the formation of the Football Alliance League. Wednesday official John Holmes was appointed president of the fledgling league. Eleven other clubs joined the competition: Birmingham St. George, Bootle, Crewe Alexandra, Darwen, Grimsby Town, Long Eaton Rangers, Newton Heath (*Manchester United*), Nottingham Forest, Small Heath (*Birmingham City*), Sunderland Albion and Walsall Town Swifts.

Wednesday duly enjoyed a tremendous first season in the league, winning all eleven homes games en route to lifting the inaugural title. Only two seasons after moving into their new Olive Grove home, Wednesday beat Bootle 2-1 on September 7th 1889 to start their new adventure. Goalkeeper Jim Smith, captain Billy Betts and defender Jack Dungworth were all ever present in that debut season as the championship was won by four points from surprise runners-up Bootle.

1889/90		P	W	D	L	F	A	Pts
1	Wednesday	22	15	2	5	70	39	32
2	Bootle	22	13	2	7	66	39	28
3	Sunderland Albion	21	12	2	7	64	39	26
4	Grimsby Town	22	12	2	8	58	47	26
5	Crewe Alexandra	22	11	2	9	68	59	24
6	Darwen	22	10	2	10	70	75	22
7	Birmingham St G	21	9	3	9	62	49	21
8	Newton Heath	22	9	2	11	40	44	20
9	Walsall Town	22	8	3	11	44	59	19
10	Small Heath	22	6	5	11	44	67	17
11	Nottingham Forest	22	6	5	11	31	62	17
12	Long Eaton	22	4	2	16	35	73	10

The new league was well received by Wednesday fans and Olive Grove crowds increased by almost 50% in the season that followed, despite the fact that their side finished with the wooden spoon, winning only four games in a hugely disappointing campaign. The previous season's bottom side, Long Eaton, had been replaced by Stoke FC while Harry 'Toddles' Woolhouse was the nearest to being ever present for the club, missing just one game.

The 1891/92 season proved not only the last for Wednesday in the league but also the last season of competition as a rival to the Football League when it effectively became its second division. New boys included the forerunner of Manchester City (Ardwick FC), Burton Swifts and Lincoln City while crowds continued to flourish at Wednesday – the Owls' average rising to almost 8,000 – as the club posted a final position of fourth to close the curtain on their pre-league days. The final game in the FAL for Wednesday came at Olive Grove on March 26th 1892 when Birmingham St. George (in their final game before disbanding) were beaten 4-0. The third and last title was won by Nottingham Forest who, along with Wednesday and Newton Heath, were voted direct into the Football League First Division.

	P	W	D	L	F	A	Pts
Alliance League	66	31	11	24	175	140	73

Biggest win .... 9-1 v Long Eaton Rangers (h) 1889/90
.... 9-1 v Small Heath (h) 1889/90
Biggest defeat .... 7-1 v Darwen (a) 1890/91
.... 7-1 v Small Heath (a) 1890/91

Most Appearances

60 .... Billy Betts
58 .... Albert Mumford
57 .... Jim Smith
49 .... Tom Cawley
45 .... Harry Woolhouse

CAN I HAVE A FLAKE IN THAT MISTER?

Right-winger Len Massarella was certainly popular at Hillsborough in the 1930s, as he was often known to turn up for training in his family's ice cream van, crammed full of goodies! In addition to the ice cream business, his family were also well known breeders of racehorses and was so large that they were able to enter a team in the Doncaster Thursday Amateur League – once going two seasons unbeaten with free scoring Len in the side!

RECORD BREAKER

The Wednesday career of French attacker Mickael Antoine-Curier lasted a mere 11 minutes; he replaced Brian Barry-Murphy after 79 minutes of the 0-0 Second Division home game against Luton Town in November 2003. He had signed on a non-contract basis the previous day and only remained on the Owls' books until the middle of December before being released. His time at Hillsborough was certainly not memorable but his feat during the 2003/04 season entered the record books as Wednesday were one of an astonishing six teams he played for in English league football. He started the season at Oldham Athletic – scoring against Wednesday at Hillsborough – and then turned out for Kidderminster Harriers and Rochdale before being signed by Wednesday boss Chris Turner. After leaving the Owls he appeared for both Notts County and Grimsby Town, setting a record that will be extremely difficult to beat!

MIND THAT FOR YOU MISTER?

In the club's amateur days Wednesday, of course, could not provide any facilities for their players with stalwart Charles Clegg remembering that he had to change under a hedge and giving a boy a few coppers to mind his clothes!

AWAY DAY BLUES

The almost constant struggles of the 1970s tested the resolve of many a supporter but those fans that travelled regularly to watch their side away from home had an even leaner time. After winning at Southampton on December 28th 1974, the Owls failed to win away again all season as the club slid disastrously into the Third Division for the first time. Hopes that the club's poor away record would improve significantly in the lower tier proved sadly incorrect as Wednesday proceeded to play 23 away games in the Third Division and register no wins whatsoever! The Owls managed ten draws, though, helping to stave off a second successive relegation – just – but it wasn't until October 16th 1976 that the barren run would finally end; Jeff Johnson netted the only goal in a victory at Reading to end the sequence at the 36th attempt. Incredibly, Wednesday then won 3-1 at Bury and 2-1 at Peterborough United, in their next away games, and were unbeaten until losing at Mansfield Town in January 1977.

TWIN

Only one set of twin brothers has recorded senior appearances for Sheffield Wednesday. Born at Stalybridge on June 4th 1935, Derek and Eric Wilkinson both arrived at Hillsborough from Duckinfield Town. Derek signed in November 1953 for £100 and his sibling arrived almost five years later, transferring across the Pennines in March 1958. Right-winger Derek proved to be the better player of the two with Wednesday having to fend off competition from the likes of Manchester United to secure his signature. After being a virtual ever-present in the club's reserve team in the mid-1950s, he eventually became a first team regular as the decade came to a close and would amass 231 appearances for Wednesday – scoring 57 goals – before a serious groin injury forced his early retirement in May 1965. He later worked as a French polisher for thirteen years before driving a forklift truck until retirement. His brother, who plied his trade on the opposite wing to Derek, signed professional forms after a successful trial at Hillsborough and became a regular in Central League football. Standing only 5ft 5ins. tall, the diminutive Eric would play only one senior game for the club. The match at Sunderland in September 1958 created club history as he appeared beside his brother – the first and so far only time twin siblings have played in a senior game together. After the 3-3 draw on Wearside, Eric struggled to secure a second chance in league football and was released at the end of the 1958/59 campaign – giving up football altogether to work as an engineer.

FIRST SUB

Substitutes were introduced into the English game in the summer of 1965, although under the stipulation that the new facility was only to be used to replace injured players. The club's first number 12, on the opening day at Manchester United, was Wilf Smith but he failed to take the field and, rather fittingly, it would be the 12th game of the season before Wednesday took advantage of the new rule. After just eight minutes of the home game with Sunderland, Don Megson retired injured and on trotted David Ford to make a little piece of Wednesday history. The Owls made a total of seven substitutions in that first season with John Quinn heading the list with four appearances.

OUT OF THE BLOCKS

The Owls' start to the 1931/32 season suggested that a third title in four years would be a formality as the club hit 20 goals in winning the first four games! An astonishing opening-day 6-1 win at Blackburn Rovers set the tone – inside-left George Stephenson netted four – before a brace from wing wizard Ellis Rimmer helped Wednesday to beat Grimsby Town 4-1 in the first home game. Five days later Bolton Wanderers were thrashed 7-1 at Hillsborough – five different men found the net – before the terrific start continued with a 3-2 win at Chelsea. The run ended in spectacular fashion with a 4-0 drubbing at Middlesbrough and a defeat at Newcastle in late September meant Wednesday lost top spot and never regained that lofty position, eventually finishing third after scoring 96 goals.

BOGEY GROUND

Wednesday were undefeated in the league against Manchester City at Hillsborough for 53 years from their first game in 1900. The run stretched to 28 games (21 wins) before City won 4-2 in 1954. In 48 games in Sheffield, Wednesday have won 30, with the points going over the Pennines five times.

FIFA TROUBLE

Wednesday's dreadlocked Dutch winger Regi Blinker found himself in hot water in November 1996 when he was banned by Fifa, while they investigated claims by Italian club Udinese that he had signed a 'declaration of intent' to sign for them when his contract at Feyenoord was due to expire in the summer of 1996. His club had, instead, took the Owls' reported offer of £275,000 for his services in March 1996. Regi scored twice on his debut in a 3-2 defeat at Aston Villa. Two weeks later his ban was lifted by the game's governing body, as the Italian club was charged with improper conduct and the Dutch winger was fined 75,000 Swiss francs (£37,500).

IRISH EYES ARE SMILING

With a total of 50 caps, full-back Nigel Worthington tops the list of international honours won whilst an Owls player. Top of the pile for the other 'home nations' are: Ron Springett (England – 33 caps), John Sheridan (Eire – 29 caps), Mark Pembridge (Wales – 17 caps) and Andrew Wilson (Scotland – 6 caps).

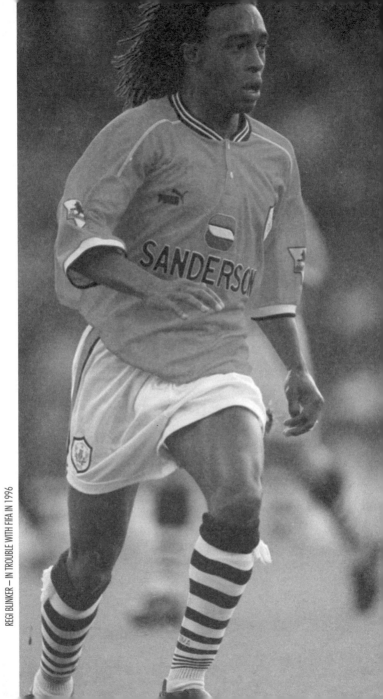

PLAYER OF THE YEAR

The annual award was started by the Sheffield Wednesday Supporters Club in 1969 with John Ritchie the first recipient. He was sold to Stoke City a few weeks later and the second winner, Peter Eustace, was not even at the club to receive the award having been sold to West Ham United in January 1970! It was third time lucky with the 1971 award as Peter Grummitt had not left, and was not about to leave. The Supporters Club continued to award the prize into the 1990s but in recent years, the winner has been decided through votes on the club's official website. Past winners have included Tommy Craig, Mick Prendergast, Eric Potts (twice), Tommy Tynan, Mark Smith, Gary Bannister, Martin Hodge, Lee Chapman and Mel Sterland. The last 20 winners are listed below:

Year	Winner
1989	Lawrie Madden
1990	David Hirst
1991	Nigel Pearson
1992	Phil King
1993	Chris Waddle
1994	Des Walker
1995	Peter Atherton
1996	Peter Atherton
1997	Des Walker
1998	Paolo Di Canio
1999	Emerson Thome
2000	Niclas Alexandersson
2001	Gerald Sibon
2002	Derek Geary
2003	Alan Quinn
2004	Guylain Ndumbu-Nsungu
2005	Steve MacLean
2006	Graham Coughlan
2007	Glenn Whelan
2008	Mark Beevers
2009	Marcus Tudgay
2010	Lee Grant

FOR CHARITY'S SAKE

The modern-day Community Shield evolved from the Sheriff of London Charity Shield, which was introduced in the 1898/99 season. The format matched the leading amateur club against the leading professional club with Wednesday invited to contest the trophy in April 1905 against the Corinthians at Crystal Palace – winning 2-1 with a double from Andrew Wilson. When the leading amateur clubs fell out with the FA in 1908, the Sheriff of London Shield was replaced by the Football Association Charity Shield, which pitched the previous season's Football League champions against the Southern League champions – Manchester United beating QPR 4-0 in the replay of the inaugural Charity Shield. Early winners included Brighton & Hove Albion and Newcastle United although in several seasons professional and amateur select teams replaced the club sides. The format settled into the current league champions versus FA Cup winners in 1930 with the Owls losing 2-1 to Arsenal (Burgess penalty) at Stamford Bridge. Five years later Wednesday were back, this time as FA Cup holders, and won the trophy for the only time in their history – a goal from Neil Dewar after 48 minutes being enough to beat Arsenal 1-0 at Highbury on October 23rd 1935. It wasn't until 1974 that the match was switched to Wembley with Cardiff's Millennium Stadium being the 19th different venue used for the competition when games were moved in 2001, as the new Wembley was being constructed.

HONG KONG PHOOEY

During the club's post season tour of south-east Asia in 1966, Wednesday played twice in the Hong Kong Stadium. A crowd of 18,000 watched them beat a local select side 2-1 in the first game, played on May 27th 1966, although the win was by no means comfortable as an Ip Kam-Hung effort hit the bar before the home goalie let a David Ford shot slip through his hands to give the Owls a lead at the break. An own goal from John Quinn levelled matters before Sam Ellis hit the winner, although Jim McCalliog was then sent off, for retaliation, before the home side hit the woodwork again. Five days later the Owls' opponents were English side Fulham – in front of 16,000 fans – and Wednesday delighted the locals by racing away to win 5-2 with David Ford (2), Graham Pugh, John Quinn and Peter Eustace finding the net.

THE TEN-YEAR SWANSONG

When forward John Pearson was sold to Charlton Athletic in May 1985, he probably thought he would not add to his tally of 27 goals in 128 games for the club. He probably thought it was even more unlikely ten years later after being released by Cardiff City. However, in June 1995 he was one of several players signed on a one-game emergency contract after Wednesday, under pressure from Uefa, decided to enter the Intertoto Cup. With a game against FC Basle in Switzerland fixed for June 24th, the Owls only had one minor problem – they had no senior players! With the first team squad all away, Wednesday had no choice but to send a virtual scratch side, containing youngsters and a smattering of seasoned professionals. Therefore, over ten years after his last appearance for the club, John Pearson added a further game to his tally, playing 90 minutes as a rag-tag Wednesday side narrowly lost 1-0.

FORTRESS HILLSBOROUGH – 2

After losing 1-0 at home to Derby County on December 13th 1902, Wednesday didn't taste defeat again at Hillsborough until Woolwich Arsenal won 3-0 on October 29th 1904 – a run of 31 First Division games. That record at home certainly contributed greatly to the back-to-back league titles won in 1902 and 1903. That record almost fell during the club's 'golden years' when Wednesday again registered consecutive First Division championships in 1929 and 1930. The run started on February 11th 1928, when Middlesbrough won 3-0 at Hillsborough, and reached 29 games after Bolton Wanderers were beaten 1-0 in the opening game of the 1930/31 season. However, Arsenal won 2-0 in the next home game to end hopes of beating the old mark.

HAPPY CHRISTMAS

For several decades Football League clubs would regularly play football on Christmas Day, usually with an early morning kick off. Just before the Great War, Wednesday had engagements down in London while in 1937 the team (plus any diehard fans) were asked to fulfil a Second Division game all the way down at Plymouth – in Devon! The 6-2 home loss to Blackpool in 1924 stood as the Owls' worst home defeat until 1992, while the 1951 game against Forest attracted 61,187 to Hillsborough, one of the largest gates for a league game in the club's history. The Christmas Day fixtures died out in the late 1950s but not before the Owls had appeared in 31 such games:

1893	Bolton Wanderers	Away	1-1
1897	Stoke FC	Home	4-0
1899	New Brighton Tower	Away	2-2
1906	Derby County	Home	1-1
1908	Sheffield United	Home	1-0
1909	Manchester United	Away	3-0
1911	Blackburn Rovers	Away	0-0
1912	Sunderland	Home	1-2
1913	Chelsea	Away	1-2
1914	Tottenham Hotspur	Home	3-2
1919	Bradford City	Away	1-1
1920	Notts County	Home	1-1
1922	Bradford City	Home	2-2
1923	Coventry City	Away	1-5
1924	Blackpool	Home	2-6
1925	Bradford City	Away	4-1
1926	Bury	Away	0-2
1928	Manchester City	Home	4-0
1929	Everton	Away	4-1
1931	Liverpool	Away	1-3
1934	Birmingham	Home	2-1
1936	Brentford	Away	1-2
1937	Plymouth Argyle	Away	4-2
1946	Bury	Away	2-4
1948	West Bromwich Albion	Away	0-1
1950	West Bromwich Albion	Away	3-1
1951	Nottingham Forest	Home	1-1
1953	Manchester United	Away	2-5
1954	Charlton Athletic	Away	0-3
1956	Birmingham City	Away	0-4
1957	Preston North End	Home	4-4

PUBLIC TRIAL MATCHES

The concept of playing pre-season friendly games is a relatively new idea, only really appearing on the football calendar on a regular basis in the mid-1960s. Prior to this, clubs tended to just stage a solitary practice game at their home ground where the first team played against the reserve side. These games were open to the public with The Stripes usually facing The Whites, in Wednesday's case. The first-ever recorded 'inter-club' game was also the first match ever to be staged by the club, on October 12th 1867. In those early days Wednesday would often stage the practice games at the beginning, and end, of the season although this quickly died out as more and more clubs were formed to fill the somewhat empty fixture list. In the nineteenth century, Wednesday were creative in picking their practice match sides with Forwards v. Backs and Married v. Single being some of the variations while the club staged five Blues v. Whites games at the start of the 1891/92 campaign! The traditional curtain raiser remained the only pre-season match action until August 1953 when 4,000 fans watched the Stripes beat the Whites 2-0. A year later the ground was out of action, as the club installed their first floodlights, so no practice match was played and this proved the death knell for the games after 86 years.

LAST MAN STANDING

The Kop at Hillsborough, the traditional home area at the ground, was the last to be developed with only minor extension/improvements and renovation work undertaken from when the ground opened in September 1899 until the mid-1980s. The club then almost doubled the size of the area and constructed a huge roof, taking the standing capacity to 22,000 – over 17,500 tried the new covered area for the opening home game of the 1986/87 season against Everton. HM Queen Elizabeth officially opened the new Kop in December 1986 but within seven years, the area was seated in line with the Taylor Report. The final game played at Hillsborough with standing capacity was on May 6th 1993 when Arsenal were beaten 1-0 in the Premiership before – at a cost of £750,000 – a total of 11,210 seats were installed with over 8,500 season ticket holders sat at the Penistone Road end for the 1993/94 campaign.

GOAL RUSH

Without doubt the most amazing scoring streak in the Owls' long history occurred early in 1961 when in five games the club crashed home 23 goals. The mini-run started on January 21st 1961 when in an incredible game at Craven Cottage, Wednesday beat Fulham 6-1 in a First Division game. A week later it was FA Cup day and Manchester United held Wednesday to a 1-1 draw at Hillsborough – watched by 58,000 – to earn an Old Trafford replay. What happened four days later has entered Wednesday history as over 65,000 fans watched in sheer disbelief as United were beaten 7-2, Keith Ellis scoring a hat-trick and John Fantham and Alan Finney grabbing two apiece. On Saturday 4th February, Preston lost 5-1 at Hillsborough and the amazing burst ended at Turf Moor, Burnley a week later when Bobby Craig netted twice as the home side were beaten 4-3. It is perhaps unsurprising to learn that the 1960/61 team finished runners-up to the Spurs double side and was arguably the best Owls line-up since the war.

DELIGHTFUL DELL

Wednesday fans always enjoyed their visit to Southampton's old Dell ground with one of the main reasons being that between December 1974 and November 1997, the Owls were unbeaten – a club-record run of 14 games.

1974/75	Second Division	1-0	Potts
1984/85	First Division	3-0	Chapman 2, Varadi
1985/86	First Division	3-2	Shutt, Shelton, Hart
1986/87	First Division	1-1	Chapman
1987/88	First Division	1-1	Chapman
1988/89	First Division	2-1	Reeves, Varadi
1989/90	First Division	2-2	Atkinson, Shirtliff
1991/92	First Division	1-0	Hirst
1992/93	Premiership	2-1	Sheridan, Hirst
1993/94	Premiership	1-1	Bart-Williams
1994/95	Premiership	0-0	
1995/96	Premiership	1-0	Degryse
1996/97	Premiership	3-2	Hirst 2, Booth
1997/98	Premiership	3-2	Atherton, Collins, Di Canio

HAVE WE FORGOTTEN SOMETHING?

The second half of the January 1948 Second Division game with Tottenham Hotspur, at Hillsborough, started in bizarre fashion as there was a few seconds' play before it was realised that the Nottingham referee was not actually on the field!

WHY DOES IT ALWAYS RAIN ON ME?

The devastating floods that hit Sheffield on June 25th 2007 caused untold damage to the city's infrastructure and sadly Hillsborough did not escape as the River Don burst its banks and overwhelmed the ground; at the height of the floodwaters the playing surface was under 15 feet of water. The South Stand was the worst affected as the dressing rooms, boardroom, tunnel and hospitality lounges were invaded by up to three feet of water – leaving a watermark on all the walls – and almost a foot of mud. The club lost all power and phone connections whilst on the opposite side of the ground the North Stand was flooded – destroying all the wooden fittings – while both the club shop and ticket office were virtually swept away, the latter being temporarily re-housed in the old sports hall. Thousands of pounds worth of stock in the shop was ruined – delaying the release of the new home kit – while season ticket applications for the new season were another casualty. Thankfully insurance paid for the estimated £1m cost to repair the extensive damage with almost £200,000 spent on the emergency re-laying of the pitch. The only trace now left of the flood is a mark on a wall beneath the South Stand showing how high the floodwater rose back on that fateful day.

MARDY BUM – 2

The usually unflappable Des Walker saw the red mist descend in October 1994 when immediately after the final whistle of a Premiership game at Ipswich Town, he inexplicably head-butted home player Simon Milton. The game, televised live by Sky TV, had just been won 2-1 thanks to David Hirst's injury-time goal but ended on a sour note as Walker walked off the pitch with three points plus an automatic red card. A month later he was called to justify his actions, receiving a three-game ban and a £1,200 fine for his indiscretion.

UNDER PRESSURE

For decades the country of South Africa was snubbed by the outside world, due to their system of apartheid. This changed in 1990 when one-time ANC (African National Congress) leader, Nelson Mandela, was released from prison after serving 27 years of a sentence for sabotage and crimes against the state. Within four years his party swept to power and after 46 years the system of apartheid was finally banished to the history books. It was against this backdrop that Sheffield Wednesday were invited to visit the African country in 1992, intending to undertake a six-day tour, which would see the Owls become the first British team to play in Cape Town for 30 years. The club would act as ambassadors for the UK as sporting links continued to be re-established with the country. However, just eight days after the trip was announced it was promptly cancelled as progress in cup competitions meant the Owls were facing an early season fixture pile up. That was not the end of the matter as 48 hours later the tour was back on – the British Government applying considerable pressure to persuade Wednesday to make the long journey to the southern hemisphere. The club duly beat Hellenic FC 2-1 in Cape Town (Paul Warhurst 2) before a second match, in Johannesburg, was played in front of the first racially integrated crowd seen at the famous Loftus Versfeld stadium. Thirty thousand fans watched the second game, versus Sundowns, with Wednesday sharing four goals prior to the Owls holding various coaching sessions with local youngsters before flying home to the UK in time for a Premiership home game against Oldham Athletic.

I'M A UNION MAN

In October 1946 the Sheffield Wednesday players became the last to join the Football Players' Union – the popular name for the Association of Football Players' and Trainers' Union formed in 1907. The body eventually became the modern day PFA (Professional Footballers' Association).

FUNNY MONEY

When club officials counted the receipts from the Owls' FA Cup tie against Bristol City, at Hillsborough in February 1924, they totalled £2,604. However, this included over 15 shillings of counterfeit cash, Wednesday being left with a large bag of coins of no value whatsoever!

I'M SURE THERE IS SOMETHING I'VE FORGOTTEN...

When player Jack Hudson was forced to act as temporary Wednesday secretary in the mid-1880s it slipped his mind to send in the club's entry for the 1886/87 English Cup competition! The club therefore failed to grace the competition in what proved to be Wednesday's final season as an amateur side – the two events being not entirely unconnected.

GAS ATTACK!

During the 1890s it was policy for popular trainer 'Plumstick' Davis to take his charges for a lunchtime meal at a local eatery, called the 'Peacock'. The players were faced with a menu consisting of a 14lb steak, 16lbs of onions and mountains of mashed potatoes, all of which was wolfed down by the hungry men. The diet did, however, cause a problem one evening when the players were treated to a night at the theatre; they would often remain at Olive Grove until 10pm, socialising and keeping themselves amused after training. It would be fair to say that the onions caused one hell of a stink amongst the theatregoers and orders came down from above that on the day of a theatre visit, onions would stay firmly off the dinner menu!

CREDIT TERMS

In the summer of 1971, Wednesday became the first Football League side to offer fans credit terms, in order to finance their season tickets. A total of 16,000 season passes, priced at £7, £9 and £11, were made available to the Provident Clothing & Supply Company who intended to canvass them door-to-door throughout the city. It has not been recorded what response the sellers received when they knocked on the front door of a Sheffield United supporter!

WADDLE WIZARD

Outstanding winger Chris Waddle was the darling of Owls fans in the early 1990s, scoring 15 times in 147 games after being signed by Trevor Francis from French club Olympic Marseille for £1m in the summer of 1992. He is also the only Sheffield Wednesday player to win the coveted Football Writers' Player of the Year award – being presented with the accolade in 1993 after a tremendous debut campaign at Hillsborough.

RESERVES

Wednesday have run a reserve side ever since the club's formation, the earliest recorded second team match being played in December 1867 when the Garrick Club were beaten 1-0. The concept of league football would not come to the fore until the late 1880s so for the following two decades, Wednesday's reserve side would therefore play in a handful of 'challenge' matches against local sides. Practically all of their early opponents – with the notable exception of Hallam and Sheffield Club – have long since disappeared; Owlerton St. Johns, West Street Reform and Wadsley Asylum to name just three. The first taste of competitive football for the reserves came during five years in the 1880s (1882-87) when the club competed in the Minor Cup (the first team playing in the Senior Cup). Wednesday competed without much success with a 10-1 win at Walkley their best result. When the club turned professional the variety of opponents for the reserves started to widen with the likes of Newark, Long Eaton Rangers and Notts Olympic appearing on the fixture lists. Finally, in 1891, the newly formed Sheffield & Hallamshire League provided the club's first taste of reserve team competitive soccer, Wednesday finishing third in that inaugural season. A move to the Sheffield & District League came in the following season with immediate success and up until the turn of the century Wednesday played in several local leagues winning several honours, including the Sheffield Senior Cup in 1895 (the club having entered their second team in the competition from 1891 onwards). With a better standard of opposition required, Wednesday left the Sheffield Association League in 1901 and joined the professional Midland League that contained several strong sides, many of which would eventually gain Football League membership (i.e. Doncaster Rovers, Grimsby Town and Chesterfield). The reserves enjoyed a very successful 21-year membership of the league, never failing to finish outside of the top ten places and winning the championship on four occasions. In those days the reserves could attract some astonishing crowds – 20,263 attending the steel city derby at Bramall Lane in 1911 – while in 1923 the club moved again, this time joining the Central League. The new league almost exclusively contained the reserve sides of fellow Football League teams with the Owls drawing 0-0 at Aston Villa, in August 1923, in their first game. The club's pre-war Central League record included a title win in 1929 and was characterised by a superb home record and poor away form.

The club recorded some big wins in the period (9-0 v. Stoke in 1928/29 and 10-2 v. Bury in 1929/30) alongside some heavy losses – their record defeat in the Central League being a 9-1 thrashing at Stoke in April 1934. The inter-war period saw the individual seasonal scoring record set when Sam Powell scored 33 times in 1926/27 while Wednesday and Blackburn drew 5-5 in 1927/28 and Wednesday completed a 7-2 and 5-1 double over the Blades' reserves in 1929/30. When the league was suspended in 1939 the Owls had won their first three games but it would be another six years before the competition re-started, Wednesday achieving immediate success in 1946 as they netted 112 times to win their second title. The Owls consistently finished in the top half of the table for the next 15 years, being runners-up in 1957 and culminating in a third championship in 1961. Up until the league was re-organised in 1982, Wednesday fared pretty poorly – only twice finishing in the top six – although in October 1961 they recorded their best-ever win as Barnsley were pummelled 14-0 at Hillsborough. In 1982 the league was spilt into two divisions, with 16 teams in each – from 1923 the reserves had played 42 times every season – and this rose to 18 sides two years later. The arrival of two divisions meant the possibility of relegation and this came in 1989 when Wednesday finished second bottom thanks to just eight wins. The Owls then won back-to-back titles as they were immediately promoted and lifted the top division title in 1991. Relegation was suffered again in 1994 although 20 goals from Richard Barker helped the club to bounce straight back again. After 66 years in the league the club switched to the FA Premier Reserve League in 1999 but during four seasons of membership it was a constant struggle winning only 11 of 98 games played as they finished bottom twice and second bottom twice. It was then back into the Central League, in 2003, where they continue to play today.

Honours (Reserves)

Central League	1929, 1946, 1961, 1991
Central League (Central)	2006
Central League – League Cup	2004
Midland League	1903, 1906, 1908, 1923
Sheffield Association League	1900, 1901
Sheffield & District League	1893, 1964
Sheffield Senior Cup	1895, 1902, 1903, 1907, 1921, 1922
Sheffield Invitation Cup	1926, 1928, 1929, 1931, 1932
Wharncliffe Charity Cup	1900, 1903, 1905, 1906, 1908, 1909
	1911, 1915, 1922, 1925, 1931, 1933

RED MIST

In February 1996 Brian Laws was boss at a Grimsby Town side that had just lost 3-2 to Luton Town. Angered by his side's defeat, and a perceived lack of effort from their Italian attacker Ivano Bonetti, Laws snapped, hurling the closest item to him straight at the controversial Bonetti. Unfortunately, the nearest thing to Laws was a plate of chicken wings, which left Bonetti with a fractured cheekbone! However, it could have been a lot worse as next to the chicken wings was an anvil!

BACK FROM TWO DOWN

When Wednesday fought back from 2-0 down to win 3-2 at Southampton, on February 22nd 1997, it was, incredibly, the first time an Owls side had achieved the feat since March 1963 at Blackpool – almost 25 years earlier!

SEED OF SUCCESS

The career of 32-year-old inside-forward Jimmy Seed seemed set to end in the summer of 1927 when his club, Tottenham Hotspur, cut his wage from £8 to £7 and refused him permission to join Guildford United as player-coach. However, his club's stubborn refusal to let him go would not only prove a huge turning point in Wednesday's fortunes but also indirectly caused Spurs to be relegated in May 1928. He eventually moved to Sheffield, in August 1927, as a makeweight in the transfer of Darkie Lowdell to White Hart Lane and joined an Owls side who were preparing for their second season back in the top flight, after winning the Second Division title in 1926. Wednesday would make a terrible start to the season but with Seed becoming an increasingly vital influence they would pull off the great escape, relegating Spurs on the final day of the season. With Seed captaining the club, the Owls would storm to consecutive league championships in 1929 and 1930 and such was his massive influence on a relatively young side that his manager, Bob Brown, once said; "If you're not fit, Jimmy, just throw your shirt onto the pitch." That comment truly symbolised his importance to the Owls during a hugely successful period of their history and he scored 38 times for the club in 146 games before retiring from the game in 1931, becoming manager at Clapton Orient.

FRENCH FARCE – 2

Contender for the worst transfer in the club's long history was that of Frenchman Patrick Blondeau. Signed from Monaco, for £1.8m, by David Pleat in June 1997, the defender had two full caps for France and came highly recommended after winning the French league title with Monaco. Unfortunately, the attacking wing-back was inexplicably utilised at right-back by Pleat in a traditional 4-4-2 formation and it was obvious from the opening day of the season that Blondeau was not only uncomfortable in his new role but simply could not adjust to the fast pace of the Premiership. The Owls' terrible start to the season also would have failed to build his confidence and he was duly sent off in a 5-2 home loss to Derby County, in only his fifth game for Wednesday. His career in Sheffield was then on borrowed time after he openly criticised both the club and the city and after just one further substitute appearance he was sold to Bordeaux in January 1998 for £1.2m – Wednesday effectively paying £100,000 for each of his six appearances!

DON'T LOOK ETHEL!

It was during the 1970s that sporting events started to see evidence of both sexes performing a 'streak' across the pitch. Wednesday fans were first treated to such a sight in November 1974 when during the home game against York City a bespectacled supporter ran naked across the pitch before gleefully smacking the matchball past a bemused Peter Springett in the Wednesday net! The unnamed individual must have thought the weather was quite cool though as he left his shoes and socks on! Female streakers are less commonplace but on the final day of the 1996/97 season men's magazine *Loaded* organised a mass streak at every Premiership ground with a total of ten young ladies revealing their 'assets' prior to kick-off!

OWLS

Although it is widely thought that the club's nickname derived from the area of Owlerton it actually came into general usage after Wednesday player George Robertson, in October 1912, presented the club with a gift of a wooden owl. This was placed under the North Stand roof and after Wednesday won their next four home matches, without conceding a goal, the nickname stuck.

HIT ME BABY ONE MORE TIME

The Wednesday career of the club's record transfer signing, Rome-born
Paolo Di Canio, ended in controversy in September 1998. Bought
from Celtic for £4.5m in the previous summer, the fiery Italian had
delighted Owls fans with his sublime talent – an incredible solo goal
at Southampton in November 1997 being the pick of his strikes.
However, along with his talent came an unpredictable temperament
although his first brush with the FA was over a relatively minor issue
– Paolo being fined £1,000 for showing his buttocks after scoring an
equaliser at Wimbledon in August 1997! His next transgression had
far more serious ramifications for both player and club as the events
on the stroke of half-time in the Hillsborough game against Arsenal
entered football folkore, alongside Cantona's kung fu kick over the
fence at Crystal Palace and Beckham's 1998 World Cup red card. After
a fairly uninspiring first 44 minutes at Hillsborough the game burst
into life when Patrick Vieira and Wim Jonk clashed near the centre
circle, the former pushing the latter to the floor. However, before the
referee, Paul Alcock, could take any action a melee ensued and in
steamed Di Canio who promptly kicked Martin Keown and was then
whacked by the Arsenal defender! The referee had no option but to
send both players from the field but as he showed the red card to Di
Canio the Italian raised his arms and pushed Alcock to the floor – the
official falling over in a rather theatrical manner. As Di Canio walked
from the field – via an altercation with Nigel Winterburn – the referee
regained his feet and brandished a red card to Keown. As the players
went off at half-time all sorts of shenanigans took place in the tunnel
and it is almost forgotten now that Wednesday actually won the game,
thanks to a terrific 89th-minute goal from Lee Briscoe. It was then
time for Di Canio – who had been instantly suspended by the Owls
– to face the music as 48 hours later he was charged with misconduct
by the FA and a month later was fined £10,000 and banned for a
total of eleven games. He was due to return on Boxing Day but after
failing to return to the club in early December he was suspended
without pay for two weeks. The whole sorry episode reached a rather
predictable conclusion in January 1999 when the Italian moved to
fellow Premiership club West Ham United for a £2m fee, after 17
goals in just 48 appearances.

PAOLO DI CANIO – HIGHLY TALENTED BUT CONTROVERSIAL RECORD SIGNING

NOT ANOTHER DEFEAT!

Any hopes of bouncing straight back to the top flight, after relegation from the Premiership in 2000, were firmly dismissed early in the following season when Wednesday registered a club record of EIGHT consecutive league defeats:

> 09/09/2000....v Wimbledon (h) 0-5
> 13/09/2000....v Nottingham Forest (h) 0-1
> 16/09/2000....v Tranmere Rovers (a)...............0-2
> 23/09/2000....v Preston North End (h) 1-3
> 30/09/2000....v Gillingham (a)........................0-2
> 08/10/2000....v West Bromwich Albion (h)...1-2
> 14/10/2000....v Portsmouth (a) 1-2
> 17/10/2000....v Burnley (a) 0-1

The run ended with a 1-0 home win over Birmingham City while loan signing, Robbie Stockdale, had the misfortune to play in six of the games before returning to his parent club! The man in charge, Paul Jewell, managed to ride the storm but lasted only until February 2001 when he departed with the club is dire straits at the foot of the First Division (Championship) table – preceded earlier in the day by chairman, Howard Cully – as the club lurched from crisis to crisis. Just under seven years later, fans were reaching for the record books again as the club set a new mark of consecutive defeats from the first day of the season:

> 11/08/2007....v Ipswich Town (a) 1-4
> 19/08/2007....v Wolverhampton W (h)..........1-3
> 25/08/2007....v Charlton Athletic (a) 2-3
> 01/09/2007....v Bristol City (h) 0-1
> 15/09/2007....v Preston North End (a)...........0-1
> 18/09/2007....v Burnley (h) 0-2

As with the previous run of losses, the sequence ended with a 1-0 win at Hillsborough – a rare Jeffers goal beating Hull City – although the hangover from the terrible start afflicted Wednesday all season; the club surviving thanks to a dramatic last-day win over Norwich City.

FOOT IN BOTH CAMPS

Born in Sheffield in 1847, Charles Stokes was a founder member of both Wednesday and United. He first became involved in the local sporting scene in the early 1860s, playing for fledgling clubs such as Heeley and Broomhall, and in 1867 was on the cricket club committee that officially formed the Wednesday FC section. In those early days, Stokes was both player and committee man – he lived at Highfields, the location of Wednesday's first home ground. He subsequently became the first treasurer of the new Sheffield & Hallamshire FA in 1887 and by that time was also serving on the committee of both Bramall Lane and Yorkshire County Cricket Club. In March 1889 he was mainly responsible for calling a special meeting from which Wednesday's age-old rivals were formed. He passed away, aged 66, in October 1913 having left a lasting legacy to the city of Sheffield.

GOOD INTENTIONS...

"This will end the situation where one million hard-up football fans have to pay £8 to £9 to stand on wet terraces or £12 to £20 for a seat to subsidise the eight million armchair critics." The words of Wednesday director Joe Ashton in reaction to the newly formed Premier League's £304m deal with BSkyB in May 1992. Unfortunately, the theory did not exactly work in practice...

SPOT OF BOTHER

Like most clubs, the Owls' record in penalty shoot-outs is somewhat mixed although in February 1995 they did achieve the almost impossible feat of leading 3-0 in the post final-whistle lottery – only to lose! The game in question was an FA Cup fourth round replay at Wolves where a normal-time goal from Mark Bright had secured a 1-1 draw to force extra time. The teams could not be separated in the extra 30 minutes and Wednesday looked set to cruise through to the last 16 after Mark Bright, Guy Whittingham and Kevin Pressman put them in command in the penalty competition. However, it was not to be as, unbelievably, Andy Pearce, Chris Bart-Williams and Chris Waddle all missed for the Owls, allowing Don Goodman to send the Black Country club through, 4-3 on spot kicks.

DON'T YOU WANT ME BABY?

Wednesday grabbed national headlines in January 1992 when boss Trevor Francis invited French 'bad boy' superstar Eric Cantona for a Hillsborough trial. The brilliant but erratic Cantona was no stranger to clashes with authorities as in December 1991, whilst playing for Nimes, he had been immediately banned for one month after throwing the ball at a referee – in reaction to a decision he disagreed with. At the subsequent FFF (French Football Federation) hearing Cantona's response to the ban was to walk up to each committee member in turn and call them idiots to their faces! Rather unsurprisingly, the ban was increased to three months and at this the somewhat disillusioned attacker announced his retirement from the game, at the age of just 25. However, after being persuaded by, amongst others, Michel Platini and Gerard Houllier, Cantona changed his mind and subsequently arrived in frozen Sheffield for an initial one-week trial. His impact was instant, scoring a hat-trick in a full scale practice match, held on the artificial pitch at the Aurora Ground, Bawtry Road, Tinsley. It would be the winter weather that would effectively decide Cantona's fate at Hillsborough as his next appearances came in an indoor six-a-side game, played at the Sheffield Arena, where the Owls lost 8-3 to US side Baltimore Blast. The inclusion of Cantona certainly boosted the attendance – to over 8,000 – and he seemed set to sign on loan until the end of the season, commenting: "I am happy to be here, happy to be with a good team and good coach. I want to be very happy here. The club is completely different to France; the ambience, the contact with Trevor Francis, with all the players. They are very nice, very friendly. It is a pleasure to play here." The infamous decision of Trevor Francis to ask him for a further week's trial – as he had not seen him play on grass due to the freezing temperatures – received a definitive "non" from Cantona who scuttled back across the English Channel after claiming he would lose face in his homeland if his trial was extended. Within 48 hours he was signing for Howard Wilkinson at Leeds United and helped them win the title a few months later – pipping Wednesday in the process – and, of course, became a legend at Old Trafford, netting 82 goals in 185 games, winning four Premiership titles and two FA Cups. For Francis and Wednesday it was a case of what might have been…

CLUB HONOURS

Premiership

Best finish – 7th 1993, 1994, 1997

First Division

Winners.. 1903, 1904, 1929, 1930
Runners-up.. 1961

Second Division (Championship)

Winners.. 1900, 1926, 1952, 1956, 1959
Runners-up... 1950, 1984
Promoted.. 1991

Third Division (League One)

Promoted.. 1980
Play-Off Winners 2005

Various Cups

Football Alliance League ...... Winners 1890
FA Cup................................ Winners 1896, 1907, 1935
.... Finalists 1890, 1966, 1993
.... Semi-finalists 1882, 1894, 1904, 1905
.... 1930, 1954, 1960, 1983, 1986
League Cup........................... Winners................................... 1991
.... Finalists 1993
.... Semi-finalists 1994, 2002
Fairs/Uefa Cup...................... Quarter-finalists 1962
Charity Shield .... Winners.................................... 1935
.... Runners-up............................ 1930

Sheffield Challenge Cup ...... Winners 1877, 1878, 1881
.... 1883, 1887, 1888
Wharncliffe Charity Cup .... Winners.......... 1879, 1882, 1883, 1886, 1888
.... Finalists 1880, 1885, 1887
Cromwell Cup...................... Winners.......................................1868

STONEY BROKE

The club's final game before being elected into the Football League – a Football Alliance League match against Birmingham St. George in March 1892 – almost did not take place as the Saints secretary informed Wednesday on the preceding Friday that they were penniless and were unable to fulfil the fixture. The problem was quickly solved as Wednesday forwarded the required monies to the Birmingham side so they could pay the players' travelling expenses and play what proved to be their last-ever game. They disbanded soon after with Harry Davis moving to Wednesday, where he gave sterling service in the club's early Football League days.

WOOL NOT SILK

After reaching the 1935 FA Cup Final, Wednesday decided to mark the occasion by purchasing a set of new silk jerseys for the trip to Wembley. However, there was panic in the dressing room immediately before the game when diminutive winger Mark Hooper (a mere 5ft 5 ins. tall) tried on his new shirt and watched it almost slide off his slight frame – the shoulders were dangling around his elbows! Luckily for the Owls, trainer George Irwin had packed the club's standard white woollen away shirt and after Hooper pulled on the shirt the other ten players had no choice but to follow suit. The legendary winger had joined the Owls back in 1927 although he could easily have joined several years earlier when starring for north-east side Cockfield Colliery. He was recommended to Owls boss Bob Brown but on seeing Hooper he said; "You are far too small," to which Hooper retorted, "I hope one day I have the pleasure of playing against Sheffield Wednesday." That day arrived in March 1926 when Hooper was the star man, scoring twice, as Wednesday crashed 5-1 at Darlington, on their way to winning the Second Division championship. In less than a year Brown had changed his opinion as the club paid £1,900 in January 1927 to secure his transfer. The signing proved to be one of Brown's best as Hooper – in partnership with fellow wing wizard Ellis Rimmer – proved a vital cog in the all-conquering Wednesday side that won back-to-back league titles in the late 1920s. One of his 135 goals for Wednesday was the second in the aforementioned FA Cup Final in 1935 as West Bromwich Albion were beaten 4-2 at the national stadium.

CUSHION THE BLOW

Soon after the new cantilever North Stand was erected in 1961, the Sheffield Wednesday Supporters Club started to earn extra revenue by hiring out cushions, on a match by match basis, for those fans who liked their posterior to be comfortable while watching the Owls! However, in November 1962 the cushions got Wednesday in hot water with the authorities after David Layne's controversial sending off against Aston Villa was met with a shower of cushions from the stand – the Owls were fined £100 for the crowd disturbance with the Wednesday attacker receiving a seven-day ban. You could still hire a cushion for a few pennies in the late 1970s but after several were launched onto the pitch in the August 1979 game with Blackburn Rovers the supporters club decided to forgo the revenue in order to not risk a repetition and the FA sanction that would in all probability follow.

GET YOUR BOOTS ON SON, YOU'RE PLAYING!

When Wednesday suffered a goalkeeping crisis in February 1972 it produced a story that would not have been out of place in a *Roy of the Rovers* comic strip. Manager Derek Dooley had his two senior keepers, Peter Springett and Peter Grummitt, both out of action for at least three weeks while even 17-year-old amateur England international Steve Barrett was ineligible as he had not signed a Football League form. After the Football League refused Wednesday permission to obtain a goalkeeper on loan, Dooley had a straight choice between 16-year-old apprentice Kevin Wilson and 19-year-old amateur Trevor Pearson. It would be Pearson, an apprentice engineer, who Dooley called up for the Second Division game at Fulham. The youngster had signed as an apprentice in 1969 but appeared in only two reserve games – when called up he was playing on a Saturday for Heanor Town and a Sunday for Woodseats WMC. Described as having a 'fine temperament', the goalie was pitched into a side struggling at the wrong end of the division and he had no chance with any of the goals as Wednesday crashed 4-0 at Craven Cottage. After the defeat in London, Pearson had the satisfaction of conceding only one goal in three further appearances before dropping out of the limelight, back into local football with a story to tell his grandchildren.

MICKEY MOUSE CUP?

When 39 spectators died at the 1985 European Cup final at the Heysel Stadium, English clubs were banned from European football. To replace the lack of action the FA introduced the Full Members' Cup, which was open to all clubs in the top two divisions. The new cup was met with total indifference by the clubs and fans – less than 6,000 supporters watched the first two games in the tournament. Throughout the seven-year life of the competition it was dogged by poor crowds, the majority of fans only too happy to see their side exit in the first round! The rules also caused a few anomalies as 1988 winners, Reading, could not defend the title after being relegated from the Second Division! The fledgling cup was almost in doubt from day one as Wednesday – scheduled opponents Huddersfield Town – and Oldham Athletic all pulled out of the tournament in September 1985 after a change of heart. The competition was here to stay and the Owls debut was inauspicious as just 7,846 were inside Hillsborough in November 1986 to see Portsmouth win a dire game 1-0. Over the years the tournament was sponsored by Simod and Zenith Data Systems with Wednesday appearing in nine games, the definite highlight being the 3-2 win over Sheffield United, which set a record crowd figure for the competition, for a match played outside of Wembley:

25/11/1986	v Portsmouth (h) 0-1	7,846
10/11/1987	v AFC Bournemouth (h) 2-0	3,756
01/12/1987	v Stoke City (h) 0-1	5,228
01/02/1989	v QPR (h) 0-1 aet	3,957
21/11/1989	v Sheffield United (h) 3-2	30,464
20/12/1989	v Middlesbrough (a) 1-4	8,716
19/12/1990	v Barnsley (h) 3-3* aet	5,942

*lost 4-2 on penalties

23/10/1991	v Manchester City (h) 3-2	7,951
26/11/1991	v Notts County (a) 0-1	4,118

STEPPING STONE

During the early years at Wednesday's Owlerton ground there was no bridge over the river Don, to the Leppings Lane entrance. Fans had no choice but to use stepping stones in the river to cross the water to see their favourites play! The stones proved particularly hazardous in winter although it is also known that some fans would take a voluntary dip – especially if dared to do so!

THE GREATEST GAME?

Over the years the Owls have been involved in dozens of memorable games, from cup finals to relegation deciders; from nail-biting promotion games to agonising cup exits. However one game stands out above them all as the greatest match of all time. In August 1968, European champions Manchester United rolled into Hillsborough, packed with star names such as George Best, Bobby Charlton, Nobby Stiles, Denis Law and Brian Kidd. Wednesday had started the season well, sitting fifth in the top flight, but no-one in the 51,931 crowd could have imagined what drama would unfold:

2 mins.........Jack Whitham scored from 20 yards 1-0
11 mins.......George Best fired home an equaliser 1-1
14 mins.......Law put United ahead..1-2
17 mins.......A great run from David Ford set up John Ritchie to equalise......2-2
26 mins.......Kidd heads on for Law to score the fifth goal.................................2-3
37 mins.......The game looked all over for the Owls as Charlton fired home ..2-4
45 mins.......On the stroke of half-time, Whitham blasted home.....................3-4
48 mins.......Nobby Stiles deflected a Whitham shot into his own net...........4-4
56 mins.......Don Megson scored, but John Fantham was offside!....................4-4
75 mins.......Whitham registered his hat-trick...5-4

UNLUCKY BREAK

After 18 months, and 60 games Paul Hart left for Birmingham City in December 1986 on a free transfer. Unfortunately, on his debut for the Blues he suffered a compound fracture of his leg and his first game proved his only appearances for the St. Andrew's side. He later became a hugely successful youth coach at both Nottingham Forest and Leeds United before managing Forest, Barnsley, Portsmouth, Queens Park Rangers and Crystal Palace.

UNHAPPY LANDING

Centre-half Walter Webster was on the Owls' books in the late 1920s, signing from Rochdale in 1929. He failed to make an appearance and returned to Rochdale in the early 1930s, prior to serving in the army during the Second World War. Walter died serving his country, when his parachute failed to open as he was dropping into North Africa in November 1942.

MASCOT EVOLUTION

The huge success of World Cup Willie – the official mascot for the 1966 tournament in England – led to several clubs introducing their own mascots. The Owls, along with Birmingham City, were the first clubs to realise the commercial potential of a popular mascot – both employing the designer of Willie, Walter Tucknall, to design a character. It was perhaps no coincidence that Wednesday's chairman, Sir Andrew Stephen, was also FA chairman, knowing first hand what commercial rewards the venture could produce. The Blues were the first to launch, with 'Beau Brummie', before Wednesday introduced 'Ozzie the Owl' to the Hillsborough fans in January 1967. The new member of the nest was introduced as part of the club's centenary celebrations and within weeks small kiosks would appear around the ground selling all kinds of Ozzie merchandise, such as car stickers, lapel badges, pens, pencils, scarves and hats. The club's retail operations commenced at the FA Cup home game with Mansfield Town on February 18th 1967 with Ozzie saying; "You must wear a BOATER". The 1967 version of Ozzie sported a rather natty straw boater! Over the ensuing years Ozzie appeared less and less in print – the Owls' struggles of the 1970s not helping his cause – but in November 1992 Ozzie was back with a bang – the Owls launching the new 6ft 6ins. tall Ozzie for the Uefa Cup tie against Kaiserslautern. The larger than life Owl was a creation of Celia Margaret and gave way to a new wave of souvenirs; the added advantage of having an Ozzie that could meet and greet the young fans being an obvious boost for merchandising options. Ozzie found himself a friend in September 1994 when 'Ollie Owl' was introduced and the nest was becoming a bit overcrowded when youngster 'Baz Owl' joined the flock! 'Barney Owl' subsequently replaced all three in 2006 but Ozzie was not out of the limelight for long, making another comeback in January 2009, at the home game with Charlton Athletic. He now reigns supreme as the club's number one furry mascot, ably assisted by his young sidekick, Barney.

FINALISTS

Wednesday hold the unique record of having reached an FA Cup Final despite being knocked out in an earlier round. This happened in 1890 when the club lost to Notts County, only for the result to be overturned on appeal!

MIDDLE-EASTERN HOLIDAY

Wednesday have played three times in the region, twice in the 1980s when the senior side faced the national team of Kuwait – winning 5-2 (Walker 2, Snodin, Marwood and Chapman) in September 1986 and losing 4-2 (Bradshaw and Hirst) in February 1988. The club's youth side also faced the national youth side of Oman twice in October 1994, losing 2-0 and winning 1-0 (Bailey).

HIGH AS A KITE

Interwar years' goalkeeper Percy Kite not only holds the record of being the only man to play a league game for Wednesday whilst still on trial but also the tallest player to ever represent the Owls. The Warrington-born custodian stood all of 6ft 6ins. tall, an incredible height in an age when most football players were well short of 6ft. He arrived from non-league soccer in April 1920 and played in the final game of the disastrous 1919/20 season – a 1-0 home win over Oldham Athletic – when Wednesday were relegated from the First Division. Despite his obvious height advantage the goalkeeper, described as 'tall, slim and agile', was not retained in May 1920 and drifted out of senior football after a brief spell in the limelight.

SPOT OF BOTHER – 2

In April 1996 the club's youth side were competing in an international tournament in St. Joseph's, France. Despite winning two and drawing one of their three group games the Owls faced a play-off match for third place with French side St. Etienne. This finished 0-0 and Wednesday eventually lost 1-0 in the penalty competition but this was only after, incredibly, the first TEN penalties were all missed!

GOOD FRIDAY

Traditionally the city of Sheffield has never recognised Good Friday as a public holiday so therefore a Football League game was not played on that day until 29th March 2002 when the Owls beat Coventry City 2-1 at Hillsborough, in a match brought forward 24 hours for Sky TV. The occasion also marked the presentation – to Derek Dooley – of a golden boot to commemorate the 47 goals he scored in a single season, fifty years earlier.

CROSS BORDER RAID

In the early days of professional football, English clubs regularly sent representatives across the border to entice the best Scottish players south of Hadrian's Wall. However, such was the fervour with which these players were jealously guarded that English clubs had to undertake a cloak and dagger operation to whisk away their targets! One such trip took place in September 1891 when Wednesday secretary Arthur Dickinson travelled to Dumbarton, along with football agent John Wilson, in the hope of securing players Towie and Spiers. The small group met in a well-known restaurant and after much persuasion by the Wednesday official, Towie signed professional forms, but before the ink was dry on the contract, in burst two Dumbarton officials flanked by two or three muscle-bound gentlemen! The only option open to the 'foreign' visitors was to put their fists up and literally fight their way out of a very sticky situation! A mob had formed outside the eatery and Dickinson somehow managed to fight his way to the train station and jumped onto a train bound for Glasgow. By the time it pulled out of the station, Dickinson was bleeding from both his mouth and nose and would end up with two black eyes, in addition to various bruises all over his body. After reaching Glasgow he dare not appear in public with such a face so holed up in a hotel for two days before sending for a chemist to make him look presentable for the trip home. Suffice to say, neither Towie nor Spiers ever played for Wednesday and those days of violence slowly died out.

DOUBLE SAVE

In August 1970, Wednesday keeper Peter Grummitt achieved the relatively rare feat of saving twice from the same penalty, taken by different players. The game in question was a Second Division match at Oxford United with Grummitt initially making a terrific low save to his left to deny Brian Thompson after 65 minutes. An eagle-eyed linesman spotted that Grummitt had moved so the referee ordered the kick to be retaken. The responsibility then passed to Colin Clarke, but he could only watch dumbfounded as Grummitt leapt to his right to save again! The double save ensured the Owls held onto a slender 1-0 lead but Oxford scored with just two minutes remaining to pinch a point.

SUNDAY BEST

In recent years football fans have become accustomed to watching their side play on virtually every day of the week – mainly due to the vastly increased television coverage of the game. This was not always the case and it was as recently as February 10th 1974 that the Owls first played a competitive fixture on a Sunday. At the time the country was in the midst of a three-day working week, imposed by the government to conserve electricity, which was severely limited due to the industrial action of the coal miners. Therefore, a move to Sunday football was tested in the Football League in January with the visit of Bristol City to Hillsborough one of several switched to the Sabbath in the following month. The trial was certainly a success for the Owls as they attracted a higher than average gate (15,888) and beat the Robins 3-1 to ease their relegation fears at the wrong end of the Second Division.

BAGGY TROUSERS

The club's disastrous 1919/20 season not only resulted in relegation from the First Division, but also an FA Cup exit to non-league Darlington. After drawing 0-0 in the north-east, the Owls were confident of winning the replay, only to lose 1-0 in a game played in such a blizzard that it prompted Wednesday winger William Harvey to buy himself a pair of Corinthian 'knickers' so he could put this hands in his pockets to keep warm during the match!

DOWN ON ONE KNEE

Romance was in the air on Valentine's Day 1998 when not one, but two, Wednesday fans proposed to their other halves. A gentleman called Darren was brave enough to ask his Liverpool supporting girlfriend (Linda) in the centre circle, at half-time, with red rose in hand! Wednesday fans Loz and Paul were also betrothed on that afternoon while years later it was the turn of another Owls fan to ask for his partner's hand in marriage, although on this occasion the Kop sang out; "You don't know what you're doing". It has not just been on February 14th that Hillsborough has been the setting of a marriage proposal as a girl said "yes" at the August 2009 pre-season game with Blackburn Rovers.

DEEPDALE DISASTER – 1

The date of February 14th 1953 is without doubt one of the worst in the club's history as not only did one of Wednesday's greatest-ever goalscorers play his last match but the club chairman also passed away. On that day, the Owls were in First Division action at Preston North End but on the morning of the match news broke that William Fearnehough – a board member since October 1910 and chairman since 1944 – had died in the Sheffield Royal Infirmary, only two days after suddenly being taken ill. His death broke a link that began back in 1867 when his father, Walter, had been a founding member of Wednesday Football Club. The second shock came in the afternoon when a collision with Preston goalkeeper George Thompson left Owls legend Derek Dooley with a broken right leg. Unfortunately, that was not the end of the story as the wound subsequently became infected with gas gangrene – the organism thought to have entered his wound through the Deepdale pitch – and Dooley became critically ill. Despite receiving injections of gangrene serum his health did not improve so on February 17th the doctors took the momentous decision to amputate his leg, in order to save the young attacker's life. Even after surgery the medical staff battled to save his life and happily they succeeded; Dooley spending several weeks in hospital before returning home to rebuild his shattered life. The world of football was in total shock at the stunning events with Sheffield football having lost a player who in his brief career netted 63 goals in 63 games – scoring a record breaking 47 goals in the 1951/52 season as Wednesday won the Second Division championship. In his brief career the larger than life ginger-haired battering-ram-style centre forward had become the most magnetic player in British football – his name known wherever the game was played. His benefit match, held at Hillsborough in 1955, attracted a sell-out 55,000 crowd, such was his popularity. He later spent time as manager at Wednesday, before his controversial dismissal on Christmas Eve 1973, and spent the remainder of his football career at neighbours, Sheffield United. His feats on the field of play have become legendary while his services to Sheffield football were rewarded in 2003 with an MBE. His life story was published in the 1990s and he passed away on March 5th 2008, with a new stretch of Sheffield's ring road named the 'Derek Dooley Way' in his memory.

SHAREHOLDER REBELLION

It is not just in recent times that Wednesday have been the subject of heavy criticism for their record both on and off the field. Way back in April 1902, at a specially convened meeting of Wednesday FC shareholders, a resolution was passed stating: "Disappointment that after 10 years' connection with First League football (excepting the year 1899) the club has not established for itself a more prominent and sure position, and begs respectively to impress on the directorate the desirability of a more progressive and energetic policy". The rebels also suggested that the club should employ a full-time manager and even an assistant secretary to take the burden off honorary secretary Arthur Dickinson. The 'respectful rebellion' probably lost some of its impetus over the two years that followed as Wednesday won back-to-back league titles!

TEAM BUILDING

It is now commonplace for a business to use outdoor activities as part of 'team building' days where employees are encouraged to work as a unit and support one another. Back in January 1976, the Owls proved to be market leaders in the concept when coach, and former marine commando, Tony Toms took the club's players for a walk on Broomhead Moor, before telling the startled squad that they would be staying the night! At the time Wednesday were struggling desperately at the wrong end of the old Third Division and manager Len Ashurst, and Toms, hatched a plan to improve team spirit with a dose of overnight survival training. Unfortunately, for the Wednesday players, the night proved to be the coldest of the entire year and they huddled together to keep warm, wearing a variety of layers, including women's tights! A famous cartoon published in the *Sheffield Star*, drawn by Whitworth, intimated that the sheep had been roughing it on the moors for years but they were no good at football either! Rumours circulated that the Owls had lost to a flock of sheep, although defender Dave Cusack joked that Wednesday had actually won, after extra time. The whole exercise was, of course, one of psychology with the tangible benefit of the drastic action coming three days later when goals from Ian Nimmo and Mick Prendergast earned Wednesday a 2-0 Hillsborough win over Chester City, giving the Owls their first league win since bonfire night 1975.

BADGE OF HONOUR

It was not until early in the 1950s that Sheffield Wednesday introduced an official club crest. This first appeared in 1950 – on club literature, including the menu for the August 1950 promotion banquet, held at the Grand Hotel in Sheffield. In the style of a coat of arms, the three-colour badge (blue, orange and green) consisted of the club's initials at the top with several crossed arrows and the sheaves of Sheffield (*Sheaf field*) below. This adorned the club's programme covers from 1951-56 until the first revamp occurred. In 1956 the club not only re-designed their crest but introduced a Latin motto 'Consilio et Animis' (by wisdom and courage). The new badge consisted of a shield showing a traditionally drawn owl, perched on a branch. The white rose of Yorkshire was depicted below with the sheaves of Sheffield, either side of the owl, retained from the original crest. This 'traditional' crest served the club throughout the 1950s and 1960s – being worn on the shirts of the 1966 FA Cup Final side – before Wednesday began the search for a new 'modern' club crest in 1973. The club invited 90 art students, at Sheffield's Granville College, to submit their ideas and it was 19-year-old Bob Walker who won with his minimalist Owl, with its large round head and eyes and sharp lines. Ironically, the student was not even a football fan but was happy to be presented with a cash prize for his efforts, Wednesday making sure they secured the copyright! Described as 'Ozzie – the Mod Owl' when launched in September 1973, the logo has remained a staple of the club's badges of the ensuing 25-plus years. The design was immediately incorporated on the club's playing kit, with the colours of yellow and black predominant on the blue and white home strip. In 1985 the initials SWFC were added to the badge before, in 1995, the club reverted to a design more akin to the 1950s, showing an 'old school' owl perched on a branch, complete with Yorkshire rose and the words *Sheffield Wednesday* and *Hillsborough*, all being encased in a shield. The 1990s also saw a circular badge introduced, which was mainly used in conjunction with the club's membership scheme. The 'retro' badge only lasted until 1999 when the club returned to the 1970s with a new design of the 'Mod owl'. The original minimalist owl returned, encased in a shield, with the club's formation of 1867 featured below.

GLOBAL A-Z

Prior to the early 1980s, the Owls' 'foreign legion' was restricted to just players born in Scotland, Wales and Ireland. However, the arrival of Yugoslavian Ante Mirocevic in 1980 opened the doors and a 21st-century Wednesday side would look strange without at least one non-British-born player within its ranks. In total, 56 players have now represented the Owls, who were born outside the UK and the Republic of Ireland:

Argentina..Pablo Bonvin, Juan Cobian
Australia...Con Blatsis, Brad Jones
Austria...Christian Mayrleb
Belgium..Gilles De Bilde, Marc Degryse
Brazil..Emerson Thome
Cameroon ....Franck Songo'o
Czech Republic ....Pavel Srnicek
DR Congo...Guylain Ndumbu-Nsungu
Denmark..Kim Olsen, Mikkel Bischoff
France...................Mickael Antoine-Curier, Patrick Blondeau
....Yoann Folly, Madjid Bougherra
Ghana ....Junior Agogo
Iceland...Siggi Jonsson
Israel ....Ben Sahar
Italy ....Benito Carbone, Paolo Di Canio
....Michele Di Piedi, Francesco Sanetti
Jamaica......................................Tony Cunningham, David Johnson
....Kenwyne Jones, Jermaine Johnson
Macedonia .... Goce Sedloski
Mauritania .... Drissa Diallo
Netherlands ....Wim Jonk, Gerald Sibon
....Etienne Esajas, Orlando Trustfull
Norway ....Petter Rudi, Trond Soltvedt
Poland .... Bartosz Slusarski
Romania.. Dan Petrescu
Serbia ....Shefki Kuqi, Rocky Lekaj
Sierra Leone ....Chris Bart-Williams
South Africa ....Paul Evans, Sean Roberts, Burton O'Brien

Spain	Zigor Aranalde
Surinam	Regi Blinker
Sweden	Niclas Alexandersson, Klas Ingesson
	Roland Nilsson, Ola Tidman
USA	John Harkes, Frank Simek
Yugoslavia	Bojan Djordjic, Darko Kovacevic
	Ante Mirocevic, Dejan Stefanovic

Players not featured in the list include Australian Adem Poric (born London), England under-23 international Wilf Smith (born and christened Wolfgang in Germany) and former Sheffield boys player Brian Strutt (born Malta).

FRIENDLY LOCAL RIVALRY!

The FA Cup meeting between Wednesday and United, in February 1900, has entered history as – without doubt – the fiercest Sheffield derby game of all time. Over 32,000 fans had seen the first game abandoned, due to snow, while the next game, scheduled for the following Thursday, was postponed when a blizzard engulfed the city. When 90 minutes were finally played the teams drew 1-1 at Bramall Lane, setting up a replay 48 hours later at Owlerton. The first half was fairly even but just before the interval Wednesday player George Lee suffered a broken leg after falling heavily and was carried from the field, leaving the home side to play the remainder of the game with ten men. It was in the second half that the game really 'warmed up' as just two minutes after the interval Langley tripped Bennett and from the penalty spot Needham put United ahead. After 71 minutes Wednesday went down to nine men when Pryce was sent off after going 'over the top' on Hedley; the United player being forced to leave the field for five minutes. Tackles were now flying in from all angles and amazingly with five minutes remaining, Wednesday went down to just eight players when Bennett was unceremoniously kicked into the air by Langley, who was ordered from the field by the overworked referee! With two minutes remaining Beers netted to complete a 2-0 win for United in a game that was talked about for years in the city and described by the local press as "a game of wild excitement which sadly tarnished the image of Sheffield football".

MONEY, MONEY, MONEY

Sheffield Wednesday turnover, wages costs and profit/loss for the last 10 years:

Year ending	Turnover (£)	Wages (£)	Profit/Loss
1999	19,124,000	13,539,000	-9,432,000
2000	18,026,000	14,375,000	-2,823,000
2001	13,228,000	13,416,000	-9,072,000
2002	18,552,000	11,411,000	-387,000
2003	8,512,000	9,801,000	-8,361,000
2004	9,026,000	5,987,000	-4,105,000
2005	9,661,000	5,508,000	-3,007,000
2006	11,613,000	5,667,000	-457,000
2007	11,321,000	6,297,000	1,491,000
2008	12,317,000	7,169,000	2,217,000
2009	11,170,000	8,180,000	-3,708,000

I KISSED A GIRL

The transfer of Scottish international forward Neil Dewar from Manchester United to Hillsborough not only caused a sensation in football circles but led directly to a scandal that would lead to the resignation of a United director. The news story broke in early January that Dewar and Betty Thomson – daughter of councillor and United director Mr A. E. Thomson – had secretly married at a Manchester registry office before Wednesday had played Manchester City at Hillsborough on Saturday 30th December 1933. The parents of 19-year-old Betty – described as a girl of 'striking appearance' – did not even know the couple were courting and were totally unaware of the relationship that had started when Dewar began to lodge near the Thomsons' home. His transfer across the Pennines was believed to have precipitated matters with the couple not wanting to be parted. The parents of Betty were told of the marriage by telephone 48 hours after the nuptials but the 'secret marriage' attracted so much media attention that her father saw no other alternative but to resign from the Old Trafford board of directors. The couple honeymooned in London before Dewar rejoined the Wednesday squad for their game at Arsenal, scoring in a 1-1 draw at Highbury.

THE GENERATION GAME

When Paul Froggatt appeared for the club's youth team, in August 1969, he became the third generation to represent Wednesday. His grandfather, Frank, led the Owls to the Second Division championship in 1926 and appeared in 96 games before moving to Notts County in November 1927. His son, Redfern, became one of the greatest players in the club's history, winning four full caps for England during the early 1950s and amassing 458 competitive games for Wednesday, scoring 148 times. He emulated his father by helping Wednesday to win the Second Division title in 1952, repeating the feat in both 1956 and 1959. In total, Don Megson and his son, Gary, totalled 24 years' service to Wednesday. The duo also amassed a total of 728 first-team games, left-back Don contributing 442 during 17 years at Hillsborough. He is rightly classed as one of the club's greatest left-backs while Gary was a stylish midfielder during the 1980s, helping the Owls to promotion in 1984 before leaving for an ill-fated spell at Nottingham Forest. He returned for a second spell in December 1985 but was one of many players who had a disagreement with boss Peter Eustace during his fateful 109 days in charge, in the late 1980s. He was sold to Manchester City for £250,000 in 1989 and ended his playing days as a non-contract player at Shrewsbury Town in 1995. He then launched a career in management which has seen Gary experience many ups and downs at a variety of clubs, including Norwich City, Blackpool, Stockport County, Stoke City, West Bromwich Albion and Bolton Wanderers. The most recent father and son combination to appear for the club was father Danny Wilson and son Laurie. Wilson senior, of course, was a mainstay of the successful Owls side of the early 1990s – appearing in 137 games and scoring 14 goals – while his offspring made just three appearances in the traumatic 2003/04 season before moving into non-league football, joining Conference side Stevenage Borough in 2007. A rather more obscure father and son combination occurred in October 1954 when David Nevin appeared for Wednesday in a Sheffield County Cup tie at Doncaster Rovers. It would be the only taste of first team football for David whose father, George, spent two spells at Wednesday in the 1930s. Nevin senior appeared in only two games for Wednesday, both in the opening months of 1933, and followed in the footsteps of his father, Ralph, who also played league soccer.

CHANGE OF HEART

In the first season after World War II, Wednesday decided to advertise the position of team manager, in order to relieve the pressure on secretary-manager Eric Taylor. On January 20th 1947 the club made the shock appointment of former Celtic and Everton player, and current Sheffield United trainer-coach, Dugald Livingstone. He had been appointed to the role at Bramall Lane in the summer of 1936 and masterminded the Blades' promotion to the top flight in 1939, at the expense of Wednesday! He accepted the role during a period when heavy snow had caused several matches to be postponed and during the lull in proceedings he then had a sudden change of heart – announcing that he had declined to accept the terms offered – and would be staying at United. He was sacked from Bramall Lane in 1949 but enjoyed a long career in management, being in charge at Newcastle United, Fulham and Chesterfield, plus spells as coach for the Eire and Belgium national sides.

CUP CALAMITIES

Wednesday have spent all but a handful of seasons in their history plying their trade in the top two divisions of English football. This has given many so-called 'minnows' the chance to grab the headlines by lowering the colours of the 'big boys'. After winning the FA Cup in 1907, the Owls crashed out to lower ranked opposition in four consecutive seasons, three to clubs not even in the Football League!

Year	Competition	Opposition	Level
1907/08	FAC	Norwich City	Non-league
1909/10	FAC	Northampton Town	Non-league
1910/11	FAC	Coventry City	Non-league
1919/20	FAC	Darlington	Non-league
1963/64	FAC	Newport County	Fourth Division
1968/69	FLC	Exeter City	Fourth Division
1969/70	FAC	Scunthorpe United	Fourth Division
1977/78	FAC	Wigan Athletic	Non-league
1985/86	FLC	Swindon Town	Fourth Division
1998/99	FLC	Cambridge United	Third Division

MARATHON NOT SNICKERS

After winning replays against both Scunthorpe United (1-0) and Tranmere Rovers (4-0), the draw for the third round of the FA Cup, in December 1978, handed the Owls the plum tie of Arsenal at Hillsborough. The Gunners, surprisingly beaten by Ipswich Town in the previous season's final, were overwhelming favourites to progress but poor weather looked set to scupper the club's chances of staging the tie on the original date. An appeal by Wednesday for volunteers to help clear the pitch was rewarded and the hard work of fans made sure the tie went ahead as arranged. Arsenal keeper Pat Jennings probably wished it had not as he was mercilessly pelted with snowballs throughout the game as a bumper 33,635 crowd watched a 1-1 draw – Jeff Johnson scoring after 47 minutes in reply to Alan Sunderland's tenth-minute goal. It seemed that the advantage had fully swung towards the First Division side but the Highbury faithful had a shock in store as Roger Wylde put Wednesday ahead after 44 minutes of the replay. In fact, the lead lasted until the very last minute before a terrific volley from Liam Brady saved the day for Arsenal and denied Third Division Wednesday one of the greatest results in their history. A period of extra time could not separate the teams so it was time for a second replay at a neutral venue – it was not until the 1980s that clubs tossed a coin to decide the venue for a third game. With Britain still in the grip of an icy winter, the choice of Leicester City's old Filbert Street ground was confirmed due to their 'weather balloon' that kept the playing surface relatively frost free. Therefore, six days after the Highbury stalemate the sides re-convened in the East Midlands with Wednesday fans providing the large majority in a 25,011 attendance. The third game ended 2-2 (Brian Hornsby scoring twice for the Owls) and as national interest grew, the teams were back at Filbert Street just 48 hours later to decide who would meet Notts County at home in the fourth round. Incredibly, match number four also failed to produce a winner as a truly classic cup tie ended 3-3 after extra time. The sides were level at 2-2 after 90 minutes (Dave Rushbury and John Lowey) and the Gunners looked to have dealt the mortal blow two minutes into the added time when Frank Stapleton fired the Londoners ahead. This Wednesday side were not to be denied though... Manager Jack Charlton was a proud man as Brian Hornsby was brought down in the area and picked himself up to fire home the equaliser, from the penalty spot, after 104 minutes. The fifth meeting, again at Filbert Street, attracted over 30,000 but the fairytale finally came to an end as Arsenal won 2-0 on the way to winning the trophy in May, beating Manchester United 3-2 at Wembley in a classic final. The tie entered the history books as the third longest game in the competition since its inception back in 1871.

THE CARETAKER

Long-serving employee Harry Liversidge held the position of caretaker at Hillsborough from 1930 until his retirement, aged 76, in 1965. Throughout the duration of World War II, Harry was Wednesday's only full-time employee, his tasks including general maintenance, cleaning, seeding and cutting the playing surface, studding boots, washing and looking after the playing strip and often acting as trainer on a Saturday afternoon. If that wasn't enough, he also dealt with all the mail and answered the telephone!

TRANSFER WINDOW

Former Wednesday player Fred Laycock was involved in a unique piece of soccer history on transfer deadline day in 1925. The Owls had signed Sheffield-born Laycock in 1924, after he had netted a hat-trick against Wednesday's reserve side in a Midland League game for Rotherham Town, but he failed to make a senior appearance for Wednesday before moving to Barrow in July 1924. It was while playing for Rotherham County (the club that merged with Rotherham Town to form Rotherham United) at Millmoor against Barrow in a Division Three (North) game, in March 1925, that he hit the headlines. During the game Fred was called off the field and incredibly signed for Nelson! The incident did not go unnoticed by the Football League, who severely censured Laycock and fined Nelson £5, 5 shillings (around £235 at today's prices).

GLOSS OR MATT?

Despite heavy snow covering the Hillsborough pitch, the Boxing Day meeting with Coventry City in 1923 was played with Wednesday winning 2-0 after the goalposts were painted dark blue!

GOAL AVERAGE – THE REVENGE!

After the Owls' superior goal average had clinched promotion from the Second Division in 1950, the club was back in the top flight for the first time since 1937. However, despite beating champions Portsmouth in their first home game, it would be a season of struggle for Wednesday as they lost four of their first five matches to quickly drop to the foot of the table. Occasionally, the Owls pulled themselves out of the bottom two relegation places but they were 22nd, and last, at both Christmas and Easter. Luckily for Wednesday, the division was tight and a win over Blackpool in the penultimate home game of the campaign suddenly saw them leap to 20th.

Bottom of the First Division, April 27th 1951

		P	W	D	L	F	A	Pts
18	Aston Villa	40	11	13	16	60	66	35
19	Charlton Athletic	40	13	9	18	59	78	35
20	WEDNESDAY	40	11	8	21	58	85	30
21	Everton	40	11	8	21	47	80	30
22	Chelsea	40	10	8	22	47	64	28

There was suddenly all to play for with Chelsea visiting London rivals Fulham next while the Owls were also in the capital, at Tottenham Hotspur. A win for the Owls and a draw or defeat for Chelsea would almost certainly have sealed the Pensioners' fate and with Everton due at Hillsborough on the last day, the tide seemed to be drifting towards Wednesday. Unfortunately, that proved not to be the case as despite a fighting display, the Owls lost 1-0 at White Hart Lane while Chelsea recorded their third consecutive win, 2-1 at Craven Cottage. To complicate matters further, Everton also won, so suddenly Wednesday were back at the bottom with just one game left to save their skin! It was therefore time to consult the maths book as the respective goal averages meant that if Chelsea won 1-0 then Wednesday would have to win 5-0, while Everton were also on 32 points, meaning they could survive also. All was set for a final-day scrap for survival. Wednesday knew they simply had to beat Everton at Hillsborough to stand any chance and 41,166 roared the Owls to an astonishing 6-0 win, Denis

Woodhead (2), Jackie Sewell (2), Alan Finney and Red Froggatt scoring. Unfortunately, all their efforts were in vain as Chelsea cruised to a 4-0 win at Stamford Bridge, meaning Wednesday needed to have won 10-0 to retain their First Division place! Therefore a year after promotion was won on a superior goal average of just 0.008 it was perhaps rather fitting, although unpleasant for Owls fans, that Wednesday were relegated by an inferior goal average of just 0.44.

Bottom of the First Division, May 5th 1951

		P	W	D	L	F	A	Pts
18	Charlton Athletic	42	14	9	19	65	82	37
19	Huddersfield Town	42	15	6	21	64	92	36
20	Chelsea	42	12	8	22	53	65	32
21	WEDNESDAY	42	12	8	22	64	83	32
22	Everton	42	12	8	22	48	86	32

ROCK DJ

Pacy winger Matt Hardwick was a professional at Hillsborough during the mid-1990s. Despite impressing in the reserve side, he only made the first team squad on one occasion; being an unused sub for the October 1994 League Cup tie against Southampton. He was released in March 1995 and subsequently dropped out of soccer to launch an alternative career as a DJ. After being resident at a variety of Sheffield venues he has risen to become one of the most popular and well known DJs on the international dance scene, playing to 28,000 fans at Don Valley Bowl on New Year's Eve 2000, and was prominent in the trance music boom of the late 1990s. He later spent ten years as a resident DJ at the globally renowned Gatecrasher, appearing in such diverse places as Moscow, Sydney, Los Angeles and Johannesburg. He has also been responsible for two Essential Mix albums, produced in collaboration with Radio One, with the second just missing out to Sasha in the Dance Music Awards. While the Owls toured Ibiza in 2004, Matt was a resident DJ on the island and he now divides his time with guest club DJ slots at the likes of Ministry of Sound, appearances at such festivals as Creamfields, plus a burgeoning career as a mixer and producer.

THE NEARLY MEN

Over 920 players have appeared for the Owls in competitive football over the last 130 years but for some players the closest they came to senior action was a lonely afternoon sat on the subs' bench waiting, in vain, for the signal to get changed and take the field. The increasing number of substitutes allowed in the modern game (from one in 1965 to seven in 2009) has meant the number of nearly men has risen considerably. Below are just a few of the players to have *almost* made the team:

David Billington: Signed for £250,000 in March 1997 but made the bench on only one occasion as injury wrecked his career.

Martin Bowler: Trainee goalkeeper who was on the bench for the Intertoto game against FC Basel in June 1995.

Neil Gibson: Former Welsh under-21 international who made the bench just once – February 2002 at Walsall – and now plays in minor football.

Bruce Grobbelaar: Colourful former Liverpool keeper who acted as substitute goalie on five occasions during the 1997/98 season. After being declared bankrupt in 2002 he returned to his homeland of South Africa where he has coached several top flight sides.

John Hutton: Reserve centre-half who was an unused sub for the First Division game at Grimsby Town in August 2000. He was released a year later, dropping into non-league soccer back in his native north-east.

Jesper Johansson: Swedish-born player who joined from Estonian club Flora Talinn, on a non-contract basis, in September 2000. He briefly appeared among the subs for a League Cup tie at Oldham Athletic but just as quickly disappeared and returned home to Scandinavia.

Kenny Johnson: The earliest 'nearly man', being named number 12 for the opening game of the 1971/72 season, at Queens Park Rangers. He later enjoyed a brief spell at Newcastle United. He returned to South Yorkshire to play local football before managing the likes of Hallam FC and Buxton.

David Lycett: Forward who was on the bench for the 3-2 win against Sheffield United at Hillsborough, in the Full Members' Cup in 1989. He made one other unused sub appearance before being released in May 1991, drifting out of professional football.

Adam Ogden: Young Academy keeper who was called up to the subs' bench on five occasions during the 2003/04 season as injuries decimated the first team squad.

Matt Shaw: 6ft 2ins. Academy forward who was an unused sub for a disastrous 4-1 FA Cup defeat at Gillingham in January 2003. He later made league appearances for Wrexham and hometown club Blackpool.

Tom Staniforth: Ginger haired centre-half who was unfortunate to be on the subs' bench on eight occasions during the 1999/00 season without once getting onto the field of play. Sadly, the popular player met with an untimely death at the age of just 19, in August 2000, when after a night out in his hometown of York, he collapsed and never regained consciousness.

David Wetherall: Sheffield-born player who it could be said slipped through the club's fingers in the early 1990s. He made the bench just once, a 2-2 draw at Watford in February 1991, but after he was sold to Leeds United (in a joint £300,000 deal that also took Jon Newsome to Elland Road) he became an established top-flight player, appearing in 250 games for Leeds before spending two seasons in the Premier League with Bradford City. He remained with the West Yorkshire club until his retirement in 2008 and is now on the coaching staff.

PENALTY REF!

Little did Colin Dobson know but after scoring from the penalty spot – seven minutes into the Boxing Day 1964 First Division game at Leicester City – Wednesday would not be awarded another penalty until October 1st 1966! The run totalled 81 league and cup games and finally came to an end at The Dell, Southampton when Peter Eustace netted from 12 yards, with just two minutes remaining of a 4-2 defeat to the Saints.

SWEEPER

A supporter of Wednesday in pre-Hillsborough days, Vin Hardy was the brother-in-law of 1880s Wednesday and England international Billy Betts. During the 1920s, Vin started a one-man campaign to keep the open terraces at Hillsborough clean and tidy – before mechanisation it was Vin's horse that pulled the roller and grass cutter around the Hillsborough pitch. This eventually became a part-time job at the club with the Kop end of Hillsborough being his pride and joy – he looked after the traditional home end from the time it was nothing more than compacted ashes. It was only ill health that caused his retirement, aged 80, in 1965.

HAIL THE CONQUERING HEROES

After becoming the first Sheffield team to win the FA Cup, Wednesday received a rousing welcome when they returned to the city on the Monday following the 1896 final win over Wolves. An hour before their train was due at Midland Station, fans began to gather around the vicinity and down along Sheaf Street. By the time the train arrived at 5.30pm thousands of fans filled the streets and a huge roar filled the evening air when the London train steamed in. Before the train had stopped the recreation band started to play 'Wednesday Boys' – a popular club song of the times – and fans rushed to the players' carriage where the triumphant team held the cup aloft for all to see. After alighting the train, the players climbed onto a horse-drawn char-a-banc to start their tour of the city's streets. However, such was the size of the crowds outside the station that, to avoid any injuries, it was decided to curtail the parade – leaving thousands of fans on High Street and Fargate disappointed. After a short rest and refreshments at the Royal Hotel, on Fargate, the Wednesday party moved into the Empire Theatre where the players had been reserved seats in the orchestra stalls with the club dignitaries given their own box! As the band played See The Conquering Hero Comes the packed house gave the team a thunderous ovation and after the first act the players, officials and theatre dignitaries all took the stage to yet more applause. After various speeches it was left to a somewhat nervous team captain Jack Earp, on behalf of the players, to "thank the house very much for the very kind reception afforded to them". After saying he was proud of his team the curtain came down and after a short interval the evening's entertainment took centre stage on a truly memorable night.

TRACKSUIT TO TV

Former Liverpool player Ian St. John was coach at Hillsborough between July 1978 and May 1979, working under Jack Charlton. He left Wednesday to start a career with broadcasting company LWT (the former London franchise of ITV) and later co-presented the popular *Saint & Greavsie Show* with former Spurs player Jimmy Greaves. The programme ran from 1985 to 1992 before being cancelled when ITV lost the football TV rights to BSkyB, on the formation of the new FA Premiership.

DEEPDALE DISASTER – 2

Victory in the first two games of the 1953/54 season saw Wednesday top of the fledgling First Division table and they travelled to Preston North End in the hope of extending that fine start to the campaign. Unfortunately, it would be an evening to forget for the Owls as a combination of events sent Wednesday to a crushing 6-0 defeat. Inside a minute the Lilywhites were ahead through Baxter but the game turned decisively after twenty minutes when visiting goalie Dave McIntosh had the misfortune to break his arm. He bravely remained in goal for a further ten minutes but eventually was forced off with full-back Norman Curtis taking his place in goal. In those pre-substitute days it meant Wednesday were also down to ten men but they reached the break just one-nil behind after Curtis saved a penalty kick from Tom Finney. However, North End scored twice in the first two minutes of the second period and it was all downhill for the Owls although, incredibly, Curtis would save his second penalty of the match after 68 minutes, denying home attacker Jimmy Baxter his hat-trick. The Preston forward had the last laugh though as he scored his side's sixth, and final goal, to complete the rout.

TOP TRANSFERS

The highest transfer fee paid by Sheffield Wednesday was to Celtic in August 1997 for the services of Italian forward Paolo Di Canio, beating the previous record fee paid the previous October to Inter Milan for his fellow Italian Benito Carbone. Here is a list of the top ten record fees paid.

Paolo Di Canio	Glasgow Celtic	August 1997	£4,500,000
Benito Carbone	Inter Milan	October 1996	£3,000,000
Gilles De Bilde	PSV Eindhoven	July 1999	£2,800,000
Andy Hinchcliffe	Everton	January 1998	£2,750,000
Andy Sinton	Queens Park Rangers	August 1993	£2,750,000
Des Walker	Sampdoria	July 1993	£2,750,000
Andy Booth	Huddersfield Town	July 1996	£2,700,000
Wim Jonk	PSV Eindhoven	August 1998	£2,500,000
Darko Kovacevic	Red Star Belgrade	December 1995	£2,500,000
Dejan Stefanovic	Red Star Belgrade	December 1995	£2,000,000

EUROPEAN BAN – 1

Today's Europa League has experienced various name changes and re-organisations since its conception back in 1955 – the first tournament taking three years to complete! It started life as the Inter-Cities Fairs Cup and was strictly contested between representative sides of cities where trade fairs were held – a rule of one team, one city being adhered to. Representative and club sides both entered the early tournaments (a London side and Birmingham City were early entrants) but the rules were relaxed in 1961 to allow more than one side from one city to be included. At the time the competition did not come under the banner of Uefa and was strictly by invitation only – Wednesday being invited for the 1961/62 season. The Owls reached the last eight but a year later were involved in a storm of controversy, which caused the FA to be widely criticised from all corners of the domestic game. At the time relations between the rulers of the English game and their foreign counterparts were somewhat strained and when the Fairs Cup committee invited Wednesday, Birmingham City and Everton into the 1962/63 competition both the FA and Football League forbade the Owls and the West Midlands club from taking part – electing Everton, Burnley and Sheffield United instead, basing their choice on league positions! The fact that England would be the best represented country in Europe did not seem to wash with the English authorities and as the two sides reached an impasse the draw was even made for the competition – Wednesday being paired against German side Victoria Cologne. At a Football League Management Committee meeting in August 1962 the decision was confirmed and the sad outcome was that Everton proved to be England's only representative with Wednesday and Birmingham being forbidden to take part. Both sides were bitterly disappointed, the Owls immediately holding an emergency board meeting and subsequently appealing to both the Football League and the FA. Unfortunately, the authorities were not willing to move on the matter and in early September the ban was re-iterated to confirm a decision that cost both banned sides an immeasurable amount of both revenue and prestige plus, of course, denied fans the chance to see top-flight Continental opposition. It was perhaps conspicuous that a year later Wednesday were allowed to take up their place in the Fairs Cup and by the early 1970s qualification became automatic when the tournament was renamed the Uefa Cup, after being taken under the umbrella of the Union of European Football Associations.

SQUAD GAME

On Saturday 5th January 1957, Wednesday fielded five different sides on a single afternoon. The first eleven drew 0-0 at Preston North End in an FA Cup third round tie while almost 6,000 fans watched the reserve side beat Huddersfield Town 5-0 at Hillsborough in a Central League fixture. Meanwhile, Gerry Young was one of the scorers as the club's third team – competing in the old Yorkshire League – won 2-0 at Rotherham side Rawmarsh Welfare. A youth team – competing in the open age Hatchard League – rattled up an 8-5 win at works side Steel, Peach & Tozer while it was left to another youthful side to beat St. John's 8-0 with Alan Finney's brother, Brian, scoring four on a notable day in Wednesday's long history.

BETTER LATE THAN NEVER

Over 40 years after being part of the 1966 England World Cup squad that lifted the Jules Rimet Trophy, former Owls goalkeeper Ron Springett was told he would finally be awarded a winner's medal. The world governing body, Fifa, had decreed that all finalists between 1930 and 1974 would be awarded medals, with the precious momentoes being given to the families of players who had sadly passed away. Therefore in June 2009, Springett attended the official award ceremony at Downing Street, along with fellow squad players such as Peter Bonetti and Jimmy Greaves. A total of eleven Englishmen were duly honoured with the Prime Minister Gordon Brown and FA Chairman Lord Triesman officially presenting the medals on a proud day for the players and their families.

TRAVEL SICKNESS

Of the first fifteen league games the Owls played against Aston Villa at Villa Park they had the unenviable record of having lost fourteen, including the club's record 10-0 defeat in 1912!

RELEGATION MASCOT

Mascot for the infamous defeat to Manchester City in April 1970, that relegated Wednesday from the First Division, was 11-year-old Colin Walker who would play first team football for Wednesday in the 1980s!

SAY HELLO WAVE GOODBYE

The Owls career of former England international midfielder David Armstrong virtually ended before it really began. The bald-headed Armstrong was signed from Southampton by Wednesday boss Howard Wilkinson on July 17th 1987 and he immediately joined his new team-mates on the club's tour of West Germany, appearing for Wednesday in a 0-0 draw against Arminia Bielefeld just 24 hours after signing. However, immediately after the game Armstrong and Wilkinson had a heart-to-heart session, which lasted late into the night, with the outcome being that just three days after joining, the club agreed to tear up his freshly signed contract. This allowed Armstrong to sign for a side nearer his Southampton base (he eventually joined AFC Bournemouth), leaving the now ex-Owl to comment: "I haven't slept for three or four nights worrying and I've asked to be released. I have a teenage son at college in Southampton and we can't switch his course to Sheffield. Either I would have to live on my own in Yorkshire, or else my son will be left behind as the rest of the family moves north. I don't think either is a fair solution. I may be throwing away a lot of money, but you can't buy family happiness." The sides parted amicably after Armstrong and Wednesday were involved in one of the shortest club careers of all time!

BLIND DRAW

When Wednesday reached the FA Cup Final in 1935 their ticket allocation was extremely limited. In fact, only just over 10,000 Wednesday supporters actually applied for a ticket for the big day. To fairly distribute the precious tickets the club hierarchy decided the fairest method was to literally ask two blind men to make the draw! Therefore, on April 12th 1935, Percy Anderson and J. Hill, from the Sheffield Royal Institute for the Blind, were invited into the Owls boardroom where they proceeded to pick out envelopes from three large wooden tubs, crammed full of unopened applications. Mr Hill commented: "It is a novel experience for us but we have enjoyed our drive down to the ground in a slap-up motor car." A local councillor received a quota for the Sheffield Wednesday supporters club but what the politically correct world of the 21st-century would have made of the events is open to question!

MAKE MINE A DOUBLE

The club record for seasonal 'doubles' is eight, recorded on five separate occasions, usually accompanied by a divisional title success. When the club ran away with the Second Division championship in the 1899/00 campaign, Wednesday recorded a 100% home record – winning 17 games at their new Owlerton ground – and eight wins on the road set a mark that would never be bettered. The figure was equalled twice more before World War II, in both 1926 and 1930, with Wednesday recording 18 home wins – from 21 games – in the former season as they won the Second Division for the second time. A win at Southampton in the final away game of the 1925/26 campaign equalled the 1900 record. When Wednesday comprehensively won the First Division title in 1930 (by a modern day equivalent of 15 points) they won eleven times on the road, eight of which completed doubles. The mark was achieved again in the 1958/59 season when Wednesday went close to setting a new figure, failing to win at either Middlesbrough or Bristol Rovers in the final two away games, when a victory in either would have broken the long-standing record. The most recent occurrence came in 1984 when promotion from the old Second Division was fuelled by eight doubles with a win at Cardiff on the final day of the season achieving the tally yet again. Rather unsurprisingly, the record for doubles conceded by Wednesday came in seasons of disaster, the 1919/20 campaign initially setting a figure of seven doubles as the Owls won just seven times to tumble out of the top division. Exactly fifty years later Manchester City became the seventh side to inflict a double on a night when relegation from the First Division was confirmed.

LAP OF (DIS) HONOUR

After leading 2-0 against Everton in the 1966 FA Cup Final, a virtual unknown by the name of Mike Trebilcock scored twice for the Toffeemen as they stormed back to win 3-2 in one of the greatest cup finals seen at the north London venue. However, Owls captain Don Megson decided not to let the gallant effort of his team go unnoticed and led the Wednesday side on a lap of honour around the Wembley pitch, starting a tradition that has been followed ever since.

FALSE HOPE

The 1989/90 season started badly for Wednesday and they quickly dropped to the foot of the First Division table. Thankfully, manager Ron Atkinson then made a series of inspired signings, including John Sheridan, Roland Nilsson and Phil King, and the Owls started to play a brand of football not seen at Hillsborough for many years, the new revamped side climbing into mid-table by spring of 1990. Unfortunately, the club then suddenly hit 'the wall' and travelled to Charlton Athletic for their final away game still needing points to make sure they finished out of the bottom three relegation places. A David Hirst brace looked to have ensured the club's safety especially as news filtered through – as Wednesday fans celebrated a 2-1 win – that relegation rivals Luton Town had lost at home to Crystal Palace. However, the Charlton PA announcer had managed to mix up the final score as Luton had in fact won 1-0 with a goal in the 89th minute, meaning Wednesday would need a point from their final game of the season to guarantee top-flight status. Visitors to Hillsborough on that fateful day in May 1990 were Brian Clough's Nottingham Forest who, just six days earlier, had beaten Oldham Athletic at Wembley to lift the League Cup (future Owl Nigel Jemson scoring the only goal of the game). Home fans in a 29,762 crowd were confident of securing the solitary point required but that soon evaporated inside the first ten minutes as Stuart Pearce fired home a terrific free kick at Hillsborough and Luton went ahead at Derby County. When Luton doubled their lead the Wednesday fans fell silent but by half-time celebrations had begun in earnest as Derby had scored twice to make the score 2-2 at the Baseball Ground! As the scores stayed level in Derby it became almost academic when Forest went into a 2-0 lead at Hillsborough as all eyes fell on letter C of the club's old manual scoreboard, at the bottom of the North Stand, which remained at 2-2. Then the man responsible for updating the board crept nervously with a number 3 in his hand and when he made the score 2-3 a blanket of despondency again descended upon the ground. With seven minutes left at Hillsborough the score became 3-0 to the visitors but by now fans had their eyes glued to letter C and ears stuck to pocket radios. Then suddenly a rumour started that Derby had equalised and slowly the news reverberated around the ground, causing fans, players and management to believe the team had been saved. This seemed to be confirmed when the scoreboard changed to 3-3 and the final whistle blew with everyone in the ground believing the Owls had stayed up. Unfortunately, that was not the case as the club's PA announcer interrupted the celebrations to relay the news that Derby had in fact NOT scored against Luton – the goal having been disallowed – and the Hatters were still ahead. Yet again, on a rollercoaster afternoon of emotions, the ground fell silent and tears started to flow when it was confirmed that Luton had won 3-2 at Derby and Wednesday were relegated to Division Two. As if to rub salt into the open wound the day also saw neighbours United promoted to the First Division, effectively taking Wednesday's place! There is no doubt that May 5th 1990 would not be remembered with fondness by any followers of the blue and white side in Sheffield.

MUNICH

The tragic events of February 1958 stunned the world of football as an aircraft carrying the Manchester United team, officials and journalists, crashed at Munich-Riem airport as it attempted to take off for the third time in poor weather. The team were travelling back from a European Cup game against Red Star Belgrade and the so-called 'Busby Babes' were decimated with only 21 people of the 44 souls on board surviving. After a few games were postponed it would be Sheffield Wednesday who provided United with their first opponents since the disaster, the FA Cup fifth round tie being re-arranged for the evening of February 19th. Wednesday player Don Gibson, who had started his career at Old Trafford, was particularly affected amongst the opposition squad as he was the son-in-law of Manchester United manager Matt Busby and immediately accompanied his wife on a trip to Munich when news of the tragedy broke. Thankfully, Busby survived the crash and the decimated United side re-started their season on a highly emotional night in Manchester. As if to emphasise the enormity of the situation, the match programme for that evening's game left the United team sheet blank and almost 60,000 packed into the ground to see United win 3-0, in a game where perhaps only a few diehard Owls fans really wanted their side to win.

THE PHILADELPHIA STORY

During the club's 1991 pre-season tour of the United States, Wednesday faced the US national side at Philadelphia's Veterans Stadium. The Owls' US international John Harkes appeared against his compatriots with Wednesday losing 2-0 in front of a bumper 44,261 crowd.

YOU'RE DROPPED SON!

The amazing goalscoring prowess of pre-war centre forward Jack Allen has been well documented (85 goals in 114 games) but after three seasons of consistent scoring and two league titles his position as the club's main attacker was usurped in rather bizarre circumstances. In those days clubs strictly adhered to a 2-3-5 formation with a centre forward at the head of the attack, supported by two inside-forwards and two wingers. Therefore, when Wednesday signed centre forward Jack Ball from Manchester United in the summer of 1930, Allen was faced with a fight for his first team place – despite having scored 33 league goals in two consecutive seasons as the Owls won the top flight title in 1929 and 1930! The Geordie started the season in the number nine shirt but after failing to score in the first three games was unceremoniously dropped to the reserves with Ball appearing in 36 of the 39 league games remaining of the 1930/31 season. In those days, of course, it would never have been an option to play both of the men in the same side as Ball scored 27 times in that season as Wednesday finished third in the First Division. For Allen, he played out the season in the Central League side – scoring 20 times – and even netted seven times in a local Sheffield Invitation Cup tie against Rotherham. However, the outstanding forward would only be reserve to Ball for that solitary season as he moved to Newcastle United for £3,500 in June 1931, later scoring both goals as the Magpies won the FA Cup in 1932.

MONKEY BUSINESS

Fans in the 35,000-plus crowd that attended the February 1909 FA Cup tie with Second Division Glossop North End, at Owlerton, were treated to a rather strange sight. An admirer of the Wednesday club, based in Southampton and just back from a trip to India, had presented player James McConnell with a real life monkey. After being named 'Jacko' he duly led the team out for their cup tie, dressed head to toe in a blue and white outfit! Unfortunately, he proved a rather unlucky mascot – Wednesday losing 1-0 to their Derbyshire opponents – and from that day forth the Irishman could not shake off the nickname of Monkey McConnell. What became of Jacko is not known…

YOU WEAR IT WELL

Wednesday have always played in blue and white, although the actual design of the kit has altered, especially in the Victorian age. Early club literature, from 1871, listed the club's kit as blue and white hoops while during the 1880s a kit of blue and white halves was adopted – possibly copying the design of the all-conquering Blackburn Rovers side of the time. Stripes became the norm in the 1890s and this stayed the same until 1945 – except for a game in March 1935 when Wednesday sported a home shirt of all blue. For the Football League North campaign of 1945/46 the hooped shirt of the 19th century was re-introduced although this only appeared fleetingly before Wednesday reverted back to stripes. The biggest change in modern times came at the start of the 1965/66 season when the stripes were, somewhat controversially, dropped altogether to be replaced by an all blue shirt with white sleeves (almost identical to the one-off 1930s kit). This stayed for seven years and was seen by superstitious fans as a bad luck kit as the Owls were relegated from the top flight in 1970. The stripes made a triumphant return in the summer of 1972 and since that day the home kit has remained 'stripey' with the only deviation from the norm occurring in 1987, and then in 1995. The former year saw Wednesday introduce a 'butcher's apron' pinstripe design, to a lukewarm reaction from fans. It could also be said that there was hardly universal enthusiasm when the stripes gave way to what could only be described as a 'blue and white Ajax kit' in 1995 – consisting of one thick blue stripe down the front on a mainly white background. Since then, the home shirt has adhered to the blue and white stripes, much to the delight of the traditionalists!

THE MASTER AT WORK

The arrival of Pele and his Santos team to Hillsborough, in October 1962, saw unprecedented interest for a friendly game with almost 50,000 packing into the ground to see the two times World Cup winner and his all conquering side. Wednesday lost 4-2 on a truly memorable night with fans talking for years about the Pele penalty that saw England goalie Ron Springett rooted to the spot as the ball flew into the net!

HARD TO BEAT

After losing 4-2 against Everton at Goodison Park on December 3rd 1960, Wednesday did not taste defeat again in a league game until they lost 2-1 to Tottenham Hotspur at White Hart Lane over four months later on April 17th 1961 – a very impressive club-record run of 19 games unbeaten, including 11 wins.

ARMS FOLDED

The Owls' 5-0 defeat at Villa Park in March 1910 hit the headlines due to the onfield display of Wednesday's Irish international James McConnell and his perceived lack of effort. Contemporary newspaper reports suggested that McConnell had been an object of humour for the crowd as he strolled around the pitch, seemingly without any commitment to the cause whatsoever! Reports suggested that when Villa scored their third goal he was stood near to the centre circle, talking to an opposition player, while in the second half he supposedly stood still with his arms folded as play went on around him. When questioned about his display he admitted he had lost heart in the second half, as Villa totally dominated the play, and explained that he had folded his arms on several occasions, but only as he was cold as he played with his long sleeves rolled up. Whatever the truth in the matter it was perhaps not a coincidence that a month later he was transferred to Chelsea!

EUROPEAN BAN – 2

Wednesday were certainly out of luck during the mid 1980s and early 1990s. After the tragic Heysel stadium disaster in 1985, and indefinite ban that followed for all English club sides, the Owls could have qualified for European football on at least three occasions, in addition to their qualification in 1992, following the lifting of the ban. Their fifth-place top-flight finish in 1986 would certainly have secured a Uefa Cup spot while the League Cup success in 1991 would, under normal circumstances, probably have secured a European Cup Winners' Cup berth for 1991/92. If that was not frustrating enough, Wednesday then reached both domestic cup finals in 1993 but could only watch as the much-coveted European places went to other clubs!

WHAT'S THE SCORE?

One of the most incident-packed games in Wednesday's long history occurred on April 27th 1912, in the final match of the season. Wednesday were the visitors to West Bromwich Albion and during the 90 minutes the ball hit the back of the net an amazing eleven times while the Baggies also fired a penalty against a post. Five goals were actually disallowed but thankfully five Owls efforts were allowed to stand with a David McLean hat-trick taking the visitors to a 5-1 win to confirm a final league position of fifth.

LINE OF DUTY

During the two world wars of the 20th century, many players with Wednesday connections fought for their country with one, Vivian Simpson, paying the ultimate price. The Sheffield-born forward was an amateur throughout his playing career – mainly appearing for Sheffield FC – but was one of the finest 'gentleman' players of his era, appearing in top flight soccer for the Owls whilst working as a solicitor. The highlight of his playing days came in February 1904 when he scored a hat-trick against Manchester United, at Owlerton, in a 6-0 win for Wednesday. A serious injury forced his early retirement and his young life ended on the killing fields of France in April 1918.

BEAST PROVED A PUSSYCAT

When the Owls splashed out £2.8m for Belgium international Gilles De Bilde, in the summer of 1999, they bought a player dubbed 'The Beast of Belgium'. In December 1996 he received a nine-month suspended jail sentence after an on-the-field clash with an opponent, which left his victim with a broken nose and saw De Bilde sold to PSV Eindhoven in disgrace. Unfortunately, despite scoring ten goals in his first season, his general attitude and apparent lack of commitment ensured he was not a popular figure amongst Owls fans, especially as he seemed more concerned with his pet dogs than the club's dire position at the wrong end of the Premiership. Wednesday eventually tumbled into the First Division and De Bilde remained only one more season before returning home to sign for RSC Anderlecht, after a spell in South Yorkshire that will not be remembered fondly by either player or fan!

MILLENNIUM MAGIC

Following relegation from the Premiership in 2000, the club's fortunes continued to wane in the lower leagues with a second relegation occurring just three years later. The road back to the top flight seemed virtually closed forever when Wednesday slumped to 16th place in the third tier of the English game in 2003/04 – officially Wednesday's second worst finish in their history. In hindsight it was the draconian decision of manager Chris Turner – in releasing virtually a whole team – that would ultimately lead to the club's revival, although the former Owls keeper would not remain to see the fruits of his transfer policy, being handed his P45 by chairman Dave Allen in September 2004. It was left to new boss Paul Sturrock to grab the baton from Turner and he achieved immediate success as the new side started to gel and quickly moved up the table to challenge for automatic promotion. Their hopes of a top-two finish slowly faded and it needed a last-gasp goal at Hull City, in the final away game of the season, to clinch a place in the Football League play-offs for the first-ever time. A 3-1 aggregate win over Brentford in the semi-finals set up a clash at Cardiff's Millennium Stadium – the temporary but extremely popular venue for the showpiece games of the domestic calendar as Wembley was being redeveloped. Interest amongst Wednesday fans was immense and when the teams ran out on May 29th 2005 over 40,000 Owls fans backed the club, more than double that of their opponents, Hartlepool United. The blue and white hordes were celebrating on the stroke of half-time when J. P. McGovern fired home, but the day looked set to end in abject disappointment as Hartlepool struck back to score twice and lead 2-1 with less than ten minutes left to play. As is often the case, the game would turn on one decision made by referee Crossley who not only awarded Wednesday an 82nd-minute penalty, but also controversially sent off Pool defender Chris Westwood. The stage was then set for top scorer Steve MacLean to make his mark on Wednesday history as he was given the onerous task of scoring from 12 yards. The Scot had been on the sidelines for several weeks and it was a big surprise when he was named amongst the Millennium Stadium substitutes. He replaced James Quinn after 75 minutes and started wild celebrations amongst the 'barmy army' when he (just) fired home from the penalty spot to bring Wednesday level and net his 20th, and certainly most vital, goal of the 2004/05 campaign. The odds were now stacked in Wednesday's favour and just three minutes into extra time, Glenn Whelan fired home to put the Owls within touching distance of the Championship. The result was secured in the final minute when youngster Drew Talbot ran clean through to round Konstantopoulos in the Hartlepool goal and gleefully roll the ball into the net to start mass celebrations amongst the Owls fans. It was just left for popular captain Lee Bullen to pick up the play-off trophy to complete a great day to be a Wednesdayite. Owls: David Lucas, Alex Bruce (Patrick Collins 75), Paul Heckingbottom, Lee Bullen, Richard Wood, Jon-Paul McGovern, Craig Rocastle, Glenn Whelan, Chris Brunt, James Quinn (Steve MacLean 75), Lee Peacock.

OUT OF AFRICA

At the end of the 1960/61 season, the Owls made a trip into the unknown when undertaking a tour of the African nation of Nigeria. Wednesday played four times but after winning their opening game 11-2 the remaining matches were hard fought affairs, played on dusty, grassless pitches, and tempers often boiled over – the local police had to rush onto the field during the third game when players started to throw punches! For one player, though, the trip proved very costly as Wednesday's part-time defender Ralph O'Donnell was sacked from his teaching job after he had been refused permission to go on tour with the Owls! Thankfully, after a period of unemployment, 'Rod' secured a job as a physical education instructor in a West Yorkshire school.

THE FIRST ASHES

Wednesday player of the 1920s, Len Armitage, boasted a famous grandfather (Tom), who was in the first England cricket team to be capped at Test level, during the inaugural Ashes tour to Australia in 1877. Due to alphabetical order, Tom is first in the list of capped cricketers although his career for Yorkshire and England was relatively brief (only scoring 33 runs and bowling 12 balls for his country) before emigrating to the US, passing away in Chicago in September 1922.

WEDNESDAY OLYMPIAN

Amateur goalkeeper Haydn Henry Clifford Hill made four appearances for Wednesday during the 1934/35 season and went on to represent Great Britain at the 1936 Olympic Games, held in Berlin. He was in the net as China were beaten 2-0 in the first round of the 16-team tournament but hopes of winning a medal were dashed as Poland won 5-4 in the quarter-finals.

THE BOSS

Bob Brown	June 1920 – Sep 1933
Billy Walker	Dec 1933 – Nov 1937
Jimmy McMullan	Jan 1938 – Apr 1942
Eric Taylor	Aug 1942 – Aug 1958
Harry Catterick	Aug 1958 – Apr 1961
Vic Buckingham	May 1961 – Apr 1964
Alan Brown	Jul 1964 – Feb 1968
Jack Marshall	Feb 1968 – Mar 1969
Danny Williams	Jul 1969 – Jan 1971
Derek Dooley	Jan 1971 – Dec 1973
Steve Burtenshaw	Jan 1974 – Oct 1975
Len Ashurst	Oct 1975 – Oct 1977
Jack Charlton	Oct 1977 – May 1983
Howard Wilkinson	Jun 1983 – Oct 1988
Peter Eustace	Oct 1988 – Feb 1989
Ron Atkinson	Feb 1989 – Jun 1991
Trevor Francis	Jun 1991 – May 1995
David Pleat	Jun 1995 – Nov 1997
Ron Atkinson	Nov 1997 – May 1998
Danny Wilson	Jul 1998 – Mar 2000
Paul Jewell	Jun 2000 – Feb 2001
Peter Shreeves	Feb 2001 – Oct 2001
Terry Yorath	Oct 2001 – Oct 2002
Chris Turner	Nov 2002 – Sep 2004
Paul Sturrock	Sep 2004 – Oct 2006
Brian Laws	Nov 2006 – Dec 2009
Alan Irvine	Jan 2010 –

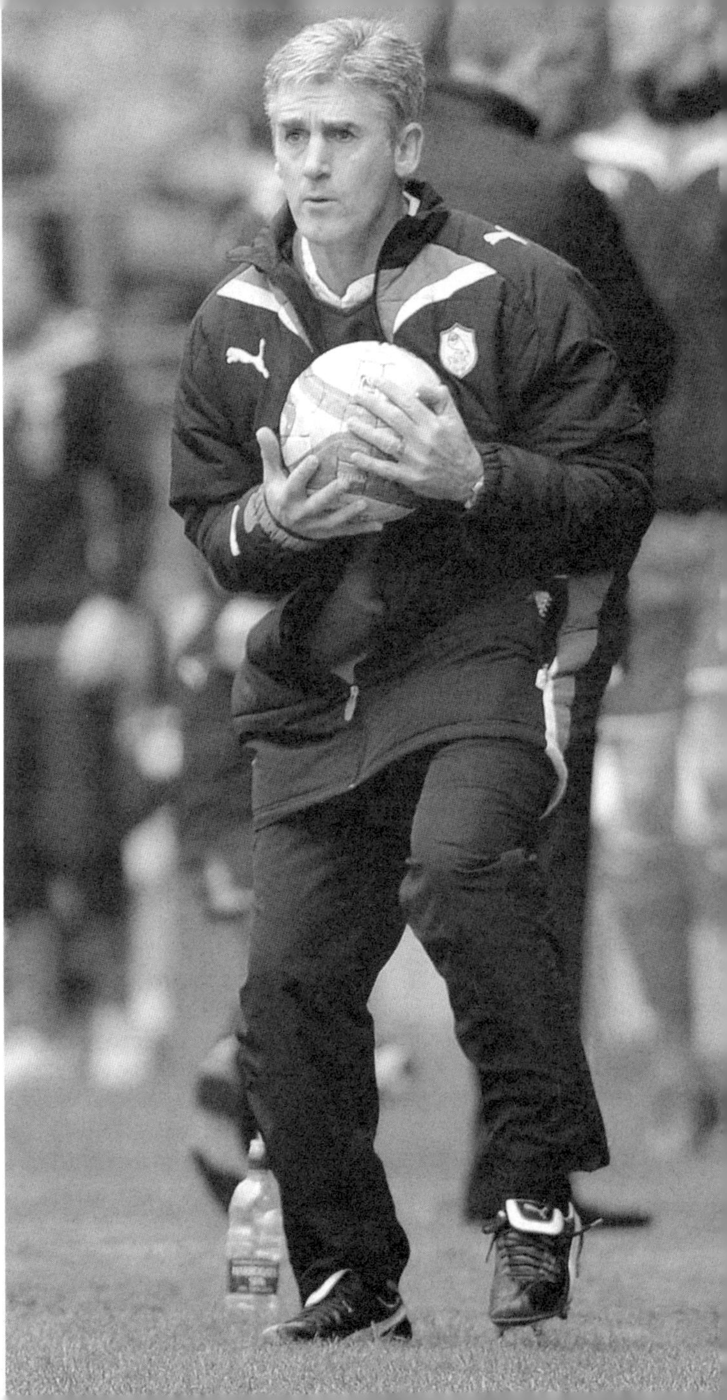

WEDNESDAY BOSS ALAN IRVINE

CASH STASH

During the club's early days at Olive Grove, secretary Arthur Dickinson would take home the match receipts and keep them under his mattress until the banks re-opened on Monday morning!

KICK A MAN WHEN HE'S DOWN

The 1970s were not a decade that will live long in the memory of any Wednesday fans as the club slowly slid down the divisions, battling against financial ruin. It is arguable that the lowest point in their history came on a wet December day in 1977 when Wednesday – sitting rock bottom of the old Third Division – travelled to Northern Premier League Wigan Athletic for a second round FA Cup tie. The biggest crowd to watch an Owls away game during the 1977/78 season – 13,871 – packed into Springfield Park and the home fans in attendance were cheering at full time as the once mighty Wednesday were beaten 1-0 to exit the competition. If the defeat was not enough for the long-suffering Owls fans, before the game they had been dropped off – in pouring rain – by the supporters club coaches outside the Wigan ground. Unfortunately, the ground was that of Wigan Rugby League club and the poor old diehard fans had to traipse all the way across town, only to witness their club lurch into another crisis.

LET'S VOTE ON IT

With the 1898/99 season due to be the club's last at Olive Grove – before the ground was lost to the extension of the Northern Railway line – Wednesday decided to gauge the opinion of their supporters by handing out several thousands voting slips at the home game with Aston Villa, in November 1898. These cards offered options for the club's new home and over ten thousand were returned, the result being:

For Carbrook	4,767
For Owlerton	4,115
Neutral	124
Sheaf House	16

The fans had made their choice but Wednesday promptly went against the majority as a plot of meadowland was secured at Owlerton a few months later!

SWEET STRIKE

When Wednesday played a friendly at Rowntree FC – a club based in York and connected to the famous sweet company – in September 1993 it was perhaps fitting that they won the game 1-0 thanks to a strike from Michael ROWNTREE!

MAN IN FORM

Forward Doug Hunt made club history in November 1938 when, in the home game against Norwich City, he grabbed six goals as Wednesday romped to a 7-0 Second Division win. The Hampshire-born attacker scored after 17, 25, 39, 44, 65 and 87 minutes and remains the only Owls player to have achieved the feat in a competitive fixture. The six-goal salvo was just part of a remarkable run of scoring for Hunt as a few days earlier he had scored all four goals in a Sheffield County Cup tie against Rotherham United and a week later bagged a treble as Wednesday triumphed 5-1 at Luton Town. He scored 31 goals in 48 games for the Owls before the Second World War effectively ended his Football League days, although he was a professional at Gloucester City after the hostilities. He later spent an incredible 28 years as trainer at Yeovil Town before his retirement in 1986.

EVERYBODY HURTS

The evening of February 4th 1987 will forever live in the memory of Owls fans that were inside Hillsborough for the FA Cup replay with Chester City. Unfortunately for England under-21 international Ian Knight, his memories of the evening were all bad as a reckless tackle from Gary Bennett – who stamped down on Knight's leg after the ball had gone – effectively wrecked his highly promising career. The sound of cracking bone could be heard all around the ground and Knight was left with injuries that physio Alan Smith rated more akin to a road traffic accident. The X-rated tackle deformed the lower part of Knight's right leg, fracturing the tibia and fibula, and driving a broken bone through the flesh. To this day, Knight's right leg is one inch shorter than his left and he was forced to retire in 1994, aged 27, after several failed comebacks – he managed four games back in the Wednesday first team in 1989 before moving to Grimsby Town in 1990.

BRIBES SCANDAL

The bribery scandal that rocked English football in April 1964 not only caused consternation amongst football fans but could also be linked indirectly to Sheffield Wednesday's demise that led to relegation in 1970. When the *Sunday People* newspaper broke the story on April 12th 1964, it alleged that two current Owls players – David Layne and Peter Swan – plus former Owl, Tony Kay, were amongst several men involved in a plan to fix several Football League games. The game involving Wednesday was at Ipswich Town on December 1st 1962 – with Swan and Layne in the side – and it transpired that the two Wednesday men had betted £50 on the game at odds of 2-1 for their side to lose – the Owls lost 2-0. They duly collected £100 each from the mastermind of the betting coup, former player Jimmy Gauld. However, it was ringleader Gauld who sold the story to the press for £7,000, therefore incriminating himself, but also the players he had enticed into the scheme. His taped conversations with the co-accused were later used in evidence and in July 1964 the Attorney General announced his decision to bring charges of conspiracy to defraud against ten men involved in the scandal. Wednesday immediately suspended the pair and the loss of top scorer Layne and centre-half Swan was a real body blow – the former had scored 52 times in just 74 First Division games and is still considered by many fans as the club's greatest post-war attacker, while his co-accused had won 19 full caps for England by 1962. The case was heard at Nottingham Crown Court in January 1965. Both Layne and Swan received jail sentences of four months and were fined £100 costs while mastermind Gauld was sent to prison for four years. On April 21st 1965 an FA commission banned all the players from either playing or managing anywhere in the world, effectively ending their careers in the game of football. It was not until June 1972 that Swan and Layne had their suspensions quashed and they both returned to Hillsborough, hoping to win contracts. The pair were duly signed but it was virtually impossible for them to regain former glories and although Swan did make a handful of first team appearances, Layne only played reserve team football before retiring. The events of 1964 were a cause of regret for both players and one can only speculate what the club could have achieved if their careers had not been ended in such dramatic circumstances.

BARTMAN

After leaving Hillsborough for £2.5m in the summer of 1995, England under-21 midfielder Chris Bart-Williams struggled to recapture the form of his early career and in 2005 ended his playing days after a short spell in Maltese football, with Marsaxlokk. In 2009 he was appointed assistant coach at US women's soccer side SoccerPlus Connecticut, whilst also helping coach the men's side at the local Quinnipiac University.

ILLEGAL APPEARANCE

The record of inside-forward Bob Curry is perhaps unique as his debut in league soccer was proven to have been illegal. The Gateshead-born attacker had graduated from Wednesday's 'ground staff' in the mid-1930s and was duly given a first team debut in a 2-1 defeat at Aston Villa in October 1937. However, it later transpired that Curry had not been registered with the authorities and Wednesday were censured and fined the sum of two guineas. The appearance at Villa Park was his only senior game for Wednesday and he had to wait until 1950 before making a legal start, playing in Colchester United's first-ever league fixture in August 1950.

WIN OR LOSE

After drawing 1-1 with Everton at Hillsborough on April 27th 1907, the Owls failed to draw a league fixture again until Woolwich Arsenal held Wednesday to the same score on November 13th 1909 – a club record run of 44 home games without a draw.

TOO LITTLE TOO LATE

After experiencing the agony of relegation on Easter Monday 2003, Wednesday travelled to Burnley for their final away game of the season and incredibly recorded the highest away win in their long history, crushing the Lancastrians 7-2! In a bizarre game both sides were forced to use their substitute goalkeepers and it would be fair to say that none of the nine goals would have won any awards for 'goal of the season'.

TOP APPEARANCES

The men who make up the club's top-20 appearance table are a mixture from throughout the club's history, including pre-First World War hero Andrew Wilson, inter-war players Ellis Rimmer, Ernie Blenkinsop, Jack Brown and Mark Hooper, long-serving Kevin Pressman and 1990s legend Des Walker. The last player on the list, David Hirst, just squeezes into the table thanks to 49 substitute appearances, therefore knocking Sheffield-born defender Mark Smith down to 21st place!

1	Andrew Wilson	1900-1920	546
2	Jack Brown	1923-1937	507
3	Alan Finney	1950-1966	504
4	Kevin Pressman	1987-2004	478
5	Tommy Crawshaw	1894-1908	465
6	Redfern Froggatt	1946-1960	458
7	Don Megson	1959-1970	442
8	John Fantham	1958-1969	434
9	Ernie Blenkinsop	1923-1934	424
10	Teddy Davison	1908-1924	424
11	Mark Hooper	1927-1937	423
12	Ellis Rimmer	1928-1938	417
13	Nigel Worthington	1984-1994	417
14	Ron Springett	1958-1967	384
15	Tom McAnearney	1952-1965	382
16	Tom Brittleton	1905-1920	372
17	Des Walker	1993-2001	362
18	Willie Layton	1898-1909	361
19	Peter Shirtliff	1978-1993	359
20	David Hirst	1986-1997	358

DEEPDALE DISASTER – 3

Wednesday struggled at the start of the 1954/55 season and matters worsened even further after a visit to Deepdale in the October. A home goal after just six minutes set the tone and by half-time the Lilywhites were 5-0 ahead. Peter Higham went on to complete a personal hat-trick in the second period as Wednesday were beaten 6-0 for the second season running.

BLUES BROTHERS

Over the years, several sets of brothers have worn Wednesday's colours, although in most cases one of the siblings achieved great success while his lesser known brother may not have even made a senior start for the club. The brother theme began way back in the early 1870s when the Clegg brothers played for The Wednesday and continued into 2010 with Richard Wood's sibling, Nick, becoming a reserve team regular after graduating from the club's academy system.

LEN & TOM ARMITAGE

Centre forward Len made three appearances for the club's first team in the disastrous relegation season of 1919/20 before playing league soccer for the likes of Leeds United, Wigan Athletic and Stoke. Sadly his brother, Tom, collapsed during a Christmas Day 1923 reserve team game at Hillsborough and five days later passed away in hospital, aged just 24.

ARNOLD & WALLY BIRCH

The Birch brothers were both born in the Sheffield district of Grenoside with goalkeeper Arnold signing for Wednesday in August 1919, after having spent the majority of the First World War interned in Holland. He amassed 29 first-team games for the Owls in the early 1920s, providing competition to legendary custodian Teddy Davison, but moved on to Chesterfield following the arrival of Jack Brown in 1923. One curiosity about Arnold was that in the April 1921 Second Division home game against Bury, he ran the line after the appointed official failed to report for duty! His sibling, Wally, arrived at Hillsborough in June 1930, from Luton Town, but he failed to add to his tally of 16 senior games for the Hatters.

CARL & DARREN BRADSHAW

After graduating through the club's youth ranks, Carl Bradshaw amassed 44 senior appearances for the Owls, scoring seven times, after making his debut in November 1986 at Queens Park Rangers. He later played across the city at Bramall Lane and in 1997 spent several weeks in jail after being found guilty of assaulting a taxi driver. Darren Bradshaw would record over 250 league appearances with several clubs after failing to break into the first team at Hillsborough, leaving to join non-league Matlock Town before finding a route back into professional football with Chesterfield.

JIM & TOM BRANDON

During the 1890s, Wednesday would utilise four members of the Brandon family, including brothers Jim and Tom. Younger brother, James, appeared in nine Football Alliance games during the period, failing to register a senior appearance, and in a relatively short Football League career he appeared briefly for Preston North End and Bootle. Tom Brandon was captain, and scored the only goal of the game, in Wednesday's first-ever league fixture and the no-nonsense full-back was one of only two players to play all thirty First Division fixtures in that debut season. However, his time at Olive Grove was soured by his acrimonious departure to Blackburn Rovers in December 1893 after 38 competitive games. He later emigrated to the US but returned home to Scotland where he worked in the Lanarkshire coalfields.

BEN, CHAS & TOM BRELSFORD

The three Brelsford brothers represented the club around the time of the Great War and early 1920s with central defender Tom achieving the greatest success with 122 appearances and six goals between 1919 and 1924. His elder brother, Charles, made his first-team bow for Wednesday in November 1912 but competition from Jimmy Spoors and then Jimmy Blair, for the left-back position, meant he could never nail down a regular place and was always a peripheral player. He was an automatic choice in wartime soccer – appearing in 88 games – but could not add to his competitive tally of seven games when the hostilities ended, leaving for South Shields in 1919. The final Brelsford brother, Ben, signed for Wednesday in November 1922 but the left-back found his way to the first team blocked by Jimmy Blair – the same player who had kept his brother in the second team a few years earlier! After two seasons of reserve team soccer he eventually moved to Barrow where he made his bow in the Football League.

JACK & LAURIE BURKINSHAW

Rotherham-born attackers Jack and Laurie Burkinshaw both featured in the Owls senior side of the immediate pre-World War I era. The first to sign was Laurie – in April 1910 – and he was joined by Jack in May 1913 when the Owls paid £150 to Swindon Town. The pair played together for the first time on Boxing Day 1913 and instantly set a record that still stands today – they are the only brothers to both score in a league game for Wednesday!

TED & TOM BUTTERY

The Buttery brothers were amateur players from the club's early days, both of whom appeared in Wednesday's first-ever FA Cup tie – at Blackburn Rovers in December 1880. Tom would only play a handful of games for Wednesday whereas his brother was a mainstay in the Wednesday side that became a force in Sheffield football in the late 1870s and early 1880s, winning countless honours.

WILLIAM & CHARLES CLEGG

The Clegg brothers were a huge influence on football's early days with the duo initially playing for Wednesday. Charles then appeared in England's first-ever international – against Scotland in 1872. Both men played together for Wednesday and became noted referees – Charles officiating in two FA Cup finals. Charles later became chairman of Wednesday (1915-1931) and was appointed chairman of the FA in 1890 – incredibly remaining in the post until his death, aged 87, in 1937. He was knighted in 1927 and throughout his life worked alongside his sibling in their father's eminent Sheffield law practice.

PERCY & TOM CRAWSHAW

During six years at Wednesday, Percy Crawshaw recorded just nine games as his older brother, Tom, became one of the Owls' greatest-ever players. In 14 years at Wednesday, Tom would amass 465 games, won 10 caps for England, and represented the Football League on eight occasions. He won both the FA Cup and league championship twice and lived to the age of 88, passing away in 1960 in Sheffield.

BRIAN & ALAN FINNEY

Left winger Alan Finney is another Owls legend who was a first team regular with Wednesday for almost 15 years. His 88 goals in 504 games places him firmly among the club's all-time greats. Brian figured in the club's youth and reserve sides in the mid-1950s but failed to make the breakthrough into senior football.

CARL & WALPOLE HILLER

A pair of 'gentleman' amateur players from the 1880s, they came from an affluent family background and played purely for pleasure, while working as solicitors. Both men made FA Cup appearances for Wednesday.

CHRIS & MARK HOOPER

Mark Hooper was one of the club's all-time greatest players (423 games) while Chris was also signed from Darlington in June 1929. He failed to make an impression on the first team at Wednesday and was soon released.

LEON & ROCKY LEKAJ

Born in Kosovo, the Lekaj brothers are Norwegian citizens. A year after signing as a scholar Rocky was handed a three-year professional contract in 2007. He featured briefly in the Owls first team while Leon has been restricted to academy and reserve soccer since joining the club in 2007.

BRIAN & JOHN LINIGHAN

The north-east-born twin brothers came through the club's youth ranks in the early 1990s. The pair became reserve team regulars but only Brian would play first team soccer – playing three games, in three competitions, in January 1994.

JIM & TOM McANEARNEY

Dundee-born brothers who both enjoyed spells in the first team at Hillsborough. Older brother, Tom, achieved greater success as he totalled 382 games in a 14-year career at Wednesday and later acted as caretaker manager. Inside-forward Jim recorded 40 games in eight years before being sold to Plymouth in 1960.

FREDDIE & JIM McCALLIOG

The big money purchase of 19-year-old Scots international Jim McCalliog, from Chelsea in 1965, not only involved the player moving north but also his parents, sister and three brothers! One of whom, Freddie, was also handed a contract by the Owls but he failed to make a senior start and was released in May 1967. Jim famously scored in the 1966 FA Cup Final; Wednesday doubled their money when he moved to Wolves three years later.

DAVID & VIC MOBLEY

In eight years as a professional at Wednesday, centre-half Vic Mobley played in 210 games and was capped 13 times at England under-23 level. His brother was signed in September 1965 but it was at his next club, Grimsby Town, that he would make his senior debut after failing to break out of the second team at Hillsborough.

BEZEK, KAZIMIERZ & STANISLAW NOWAKOWSKI

Three brothers of Polish descent who were on the club's playing staff in the mid-1960s. Only Bezek did not progress from trainee to professional but none of the trio played first team football.

ALBERT & GEORGE QUIXALL

Sold to Manchester United for a British record £45,000 fee in 1958, Albert Quixall was a star of the 1950s side. Capped five times by England, he netted 65 goals in 260 matches for Wednesday while George was briefly on the club's books in the same decade without making a senior appearance.

PAUL & PETER SHIRTLIFF

Born in Sheffield and Barnsley respectively, Peter and Paul Shirtliff both broke into Wednesday's first team while still teenagers with the latter amassing 359 games in two spells at Hillsborough. His younger brother, Paul, recorded only ten games and made his name in non-league football – winning 15 England semi-professional caps – but sadly passed away, aged just 46, in September 2009 after a long battle against cancer.

JAMIE & MICHAEL SIMPKINS

The Simpkins brothers were on the Owls' books in the mid-1990s but neither could manage a senior game for the club. Michael would play league football with Chesterfield, Cardiff City and Rochdale while Jamie dropped into non-league football.

PETER & RON SPRINGETT

The goalkeeping siblings were involved in a unique transfer when they swapped clubs in the summer of 1967 – Ron returning to QPR and his younger brother, Peter, moving north to Sheffield. The older Springett was, of course, capped 33 times by England whilst on the Owls' books, while Peter totalled 207 appearances in eight years with Wednesday before joining the South Yorkshire police force.

NICK & RICHARD WOOD

In over six years as a professional at Wednesday, Richard Wood totalled 189 games before moving to Coventry City in November 2009. His younger brother, and fellow central defender, Nick became a first-year professional at Hillsborough in 2009 and spent a spell on loan at Sheffield FC after being an unused sub for the Championship game at Bristol City in October 2009 – ironically a week before his brother played his final game for the club.

THE LOAN RANGER

In recent years, particularly for clubs outside of the Premiership, the use of loan players to bolster a squad has become increasingly important. Back in the 2007/08 campaign, Wednesday had so many loanees that they accidentally included more than the five allowed in any matchday squad when naming six against Stoke City at Hillsborough in March 2008; Graham Kavanagh, Franck Songo'o, Ben Sahar, Enoch Showumni, Adam Bolder and Bartosz Slusarski. Although only four played in the match, Wednesday were relatively lucky to escape with just a £2,000 fine from the Football League. One of the club's first-ever loan signings was Northern Ireland international Eric McMordie, who joined from top-flight Middlesbrough in October 1974. At the time the Owls were struggling in the old Second Division and the striker made a huge impact, scoring six times in nine games during a two-month stay at Hillsborough. The Belfast-born player insisted that his stay was only temporary – despite Wednesday's attempts to persuade him to move south – and despite returning to Boro halfway through the season he would be the Owls' top scorer in a desperate season, which ended with relegation to the third tier for the first time in their history. The first player the Owls actually signed on loan was West Ham United goalkeeper Bobby Ferguson, in February 1974, but during the 1970s the flow of loan players tended to be out of Hillsborough. The likes of Peter Grummitt (Brighton & Hove Albion), David Layne (Hereford United), Jackie Sinclair (Chesterfield), Eddie Prudham (Partick Thistle), David Sunley (Nottingham Forest) and Roger Wylde (Burnley) were all loaned out by the club. The club's first loan capture of the 1980s proved a real asset. After his month-long stay had ended Wednesday paid £50,000 for Aston Villa's Gary Shelton. The midfielder would become a big favourite with Owls fans and appeared in 241 games in five years at Hillsborough. Goalkeeper Martin Hodge also signed after an initial loan period but during the relative successes of the 1980s and early 1990s, the Owls actually signed only a handful of players on a temporary basis. The Owls sent many more players out of the club, to give them league experience or to facilitate a full transfer. Arguably the most successful loan signing by Wednesday came in the 2004/05 season when they signed the virtually unknown Trinidad and Tobago international Kenwyne Jones, from Premiership Southampton. His career seemed at a crossroads when Paul Sturrock signed him, but after firing home seven goals in seven games he returned to the Saints revitalised and eventually cost Sunderland a whopping £6m for his signature in 2007. Perhaps the most unlucky loan player must be full-back Robbie Stockdale, who would have been sadly wrong if he hoped a move to Wednesday, in September 2000, would boost his confidence levels – the Owls duly lost all six games in which he played! For some players, the loan move to Hillsborough did not see them even make a senior appearance. An early example was Manchester United striker Ray Botham, who joined in September 1976, while former European Cup winner, with Aston Villa, Gary Shaw spent two months on loan from Austrian club Klagenfurt in 1989 only to play reserve team soccer for the whole period. Experienced goalkeeper Tony Godden was also signed in 1989, as back up to Chris Turner, but also failed to play first team football. Early 1990s loan winger, Brian Mooney, surely holds the record of the longest time at Wednesday without playing a first team game – the Preston North End attacker joined in July 1990 and did not return to Deepdale until November, at which point he was sold to Sunderland! The first decade of the 21st century saw the Owls sign a plethora of loan men, including some well-known players and some not so famous. Unfortunately, as is the case with the transient nature of loan signings, the majority failed to make any significant impact. The following 65 players signed on loan during the decade:

Aug 2000	Ashley Westwood*, Simon Grayson
Sep 2000	Robbie Stockdale, Terry Cooke
Dec 2000	Con Blatsis
Jan 2001	Marlon Beresford
Feb 2001	Trond Soltvedt*, Carlton Palmer
Mar 2001	Stuart Ripley
Aug 2001	Pablo Bonvin
Sep 2001	Carlton Palmer (again)
Dec 2001	Dean Windass, Bojan Djordjic
Jan 2002	Paul Heald
Feb 2002	David Johnson
Mar 2002	Jon McCarthy
Jun 2002	Leon Knight
Dec 2002	Adam Proudlock, Allan Johnston, Garry Monk, Lee Bradbury
Jan 2003	Carl Robinson, Michael Reddy*
Feb 2003	Lee Bradbury (again)
Sep 2003	Richard Lucas*
Dec 2003	Richard Lucas (again)*, Mark Burchill
Jan 2004	Mark Wilson
Feb 2004	Adam Chambers
Sep 2004	Hasney Aljofree
Dec 2004	Joey O'Brien, Kenwyne Jones
Jan 2005	Adam Green
Mar 2005	Paul Gallacher, Alex Bruce, Graham Barrett
Jul 2005	Chris Eagles
Aug 2005	Leon Best
Oct 2005	Gabriel Agbonlahor
Nov 2005	Nicky Weaver, Darryl Murphy, Peter Gilbert*

Jan 2006 ....Marcus Tudgay*, Leon Best (again), Yoann Folly*
Mar 2006 ....Scott Carson, Mikkel Bischoff
Aug 2006 ....Brad Jones, Lloyd Sam
Nov 2006 ....Mark Crossley, Wayne Andrews, Shwan Jalal
Feb 2007 .... Steve Watson*, Iain Turner
Sep 2007 .... Michael Johnson, Graham Kavanagh
Jan 2008 ....Graham Kavanagh (again), Enoch Showunmi
Feb 2008 ....Adam Bolder, Ben Sahar
Mar 2008 ....Franck Songo'o, Bartosz Slusarski
Jul 2008 .... Jimmy Smith
Aug 2008 .... Tony McMahon
Oct 2008 .... Lewis Buxton*
Nov 2008 .... Tony McMahon (again), Bartosz Slusarski (again)
Jan 2009 .... Darren Potter*, Michael Gray*
Mar 2009 ....Luke Varney
Aug 2009 .... Luke Varney (again)
Nov 2009 ....Warren Feeney, Tom Soares

* Signed permanently after loan period

POINTS IN THE BAG?

When Wednesday led 4-1 (Jackie Sinclair 2, Mick Prendergast, Sam Ellis (pen)) at Hull City on Boxing Day 1970 – with just seven minutes left to play – they looked set to earn a welcome two points in a season where they struggled to adapt after relegation from the First Division. However, the Tigers had other ideas and incredibly they netted three times in just four minutes to stun the travelling Wednesday fans as the match finished 4-4.

FOGBOUND – 1

The Second Division game at Highfield Road between Coventry City and Wednesday, in November 1949, kicked off in fog and conditions worsened as the match progressed. The second half started with many fans unable to see the pitch and when home forward Ted Roberts went off for treatment it took him several minutes to get back onto the field as he could not find the referee to gain permission to re-enter the fray! Unsurprisingly, the game was finally abandoned after 63 minutes with City leading 1-0 at the time, Roberts having netted after just two minutes.

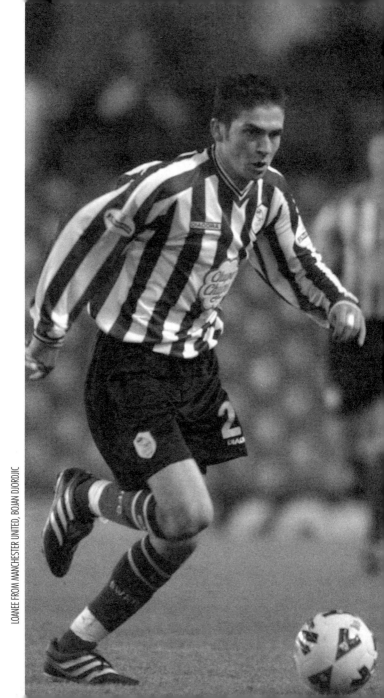

RENAISSANCE MAN

The modern-day supporter is used to multinational teams, but the influx of foreign players is a relatively recent phenomenon. In the early days of English football it was virtually unheard of for a player to earn his living outside of the British Isles. However, Fred Spiksley was a considerable exception to the rule.

- Born in Gainsborough in 1870
- Joined the Owls in 1891
- Scored a hat-trick, on his debut, for England against Scotland
- Won both the FA Cup and First Division title at Wednesday
- Refused an interview for the Watford manager's job after it clashed with a race meeting – he loved the 'Sport of Kings'
- Played the piano in Fred Karno's travelling sketch show
- Fined £2 in 1908 for illegal betting
- Declared bankrupt with debts of £84
- Worked as a freelance writer and scout
- Moved to Sweden where he coached teams in Stockholm
- Took charge of the Swedish national side for one game
- Appointed coach at German side Munich 1860
- Coach at FC Nuremburg when arrested and imprisoned at the start of World War I
- Escaped and fled back to England
- Moved to the US where in 1915 he was working as a munitions inspector
- Appointed coach at FC Barcelona in 1918
- Returned to Sheffield where he was found guilty of deserting his wife, Ellen
- Became head of the despatch department of the Mexico City branch of the Canadian Bank of Montreal (Fred was fluent in several languages)
- Coached Mexican clubs Real Espana OD and The Reforma Club
- Appointed to Fulham's coaching staff in 1924 (see YouTube)
- Won the German Cup with FC Nuremburg in 1927
- Divorced after alleged misconduct with a woman from Twickenham!
- Coached in Switzerland – at Lausanne Sports – before retiring
- Married again, aged 59, and competed in skating, rowing and swimming competitions
- After a major operation he lived in London for the remainder of his days
- Collapsed and died in 1948, during the 3.10 race at Goodwood, after supposedly backing the winner

SLEEPING WITH THE ENEMY

When Marco Haber arrived on trial at Hillsborough from Spanish club Las Palmas in April 1999, only a handful of Wednesdayites remembered the significance of the former German under-21 international. Almost seven years earlier – in October 1992 – Wednesday were involved in a controversial Uefa Cup tie at German side Kaiserslautern, where star striker David Hirst was red carded after an innocuous challenge on a home player. The player in question fell to the floor as if shot by a sniper and the French referee – who had not seen the incident – sent Hirst from the field after the home crowd bayed for blood. The theatrical German – who instantly became public enemy number one amongst Owls fans and was booed incessantly in the second leg in Sheffield – was none other than Marco Haber!

THE DAY WE MISSED THE TRAIN

Wednesday were left with a major problem in August 1923 when two players missed the 1.48pm train from Midland Station, for the midweek match at Port Vale. The guilty men were Billy Felton and Rees Williams while the shortage was partly solved with travelling reserve Charlie Petrie filling one of the gaps. This still left Wednesday with only ten men for the Second Division game at the Recreation Ground. It was left to the club's trainer, Jerry Jackson, to volunteer to make up the numbers, gamely taking his place on the right as an emergency winger. However, Jackson was certainly no 'spring chicken' and when the game kicked off he set the record as the oldest player to ever appear for the Owls. His age has yet to be confirmed but it is believed he was either 46 or 50 years old, comfortably beating goalkeeping coach Eric Nixon who made a sub appearance in September 2003, at the age of 40 years, 358 days. Unsurprisingly, Jackson – a former player with Burnley – struggled with his fitness and provided nothing more than 'nuisance value' before retiring from the field, exhausted, with ten minutes left of the first half. Wednesday eventually lost 2-0 while Jackson left his Hillsborough post in May 1924. He later suffered a stroke whilst employed as trainer at Reading and in June 1927 was tragically found dead in his Grimsby lodgings, prior to taking up his appointment as trainer to the Mariners.

BACK IN STYLE

After the traumatic, and unexpected, relegation suffered in 1990 the club remained positive in the following pre-season and Wednesday fans were genuinely optimistic that their side could bounce straight back. Playing a stylish brand of attacking football, the Owls made a fantastic start to the 1990/91 campaign, winning 2-0 at Ipswich Town on the opening day before David Hirst became the first man since Derek Dooley to score four in a league game, achieving the feat in the 5-1 win over Hull City in the first home match. The great start continued and after a dozen games the Owls were unbeaten and one of three teams still to lose:

Second Division 23/10/90

		P	W	D	L	F	A	Pts
1	Oldham Athletic	13	9	4	0	24	10	31
2	WEDNESDAY	12	8	4	0	27	8	28
3	West Ham United	13	7	6	0	22	8	27
4	Wolverhampton W.	13	6	5	2	22	12	23
5	Millwall	12	6	4	2	21	12	22

The following game, at Millwall, provided a double blow as not only did the Lions recover from a two-goal deficit to win 4-2, but Wednesday also lost outstanding Swedish right-back Roland Nilsson to a serious knee injury. The loss of Nilsson, though, gave a chance to unknown American John Harkes and the Owls continued to ride high in the league into 1991, as well as winning through to the last eight of the League Cup – beating Brentford, Swindon Town and Derby County en route. The early weeks of the New Year were dominated by those League Cup exploits. After a 1-0 win at top-flight Coventry, Ron Atkinson's troops stunned Chelsea by winning 2-0 in the first leg of the semi-final in London. Then, on a truly memorable night at Hillsborough, Wednesday completed a 5-1 aggregate success to reach Wembley for the first time in 25 years. Just before reaching Wembley the Owls exited the FA Cup at the fifth round stage but 'Big Ron' managed to inspire his troops to maintain their challenge for promotion, Wednesday still occupied one of the three promotion places with a dozen games to play... The big day at Wembley arrived on April 21st 1991 with the Owls classed as underdogs against Manchester United. What happened is well documented as a crisp 37th-minute strike from John Sheridan sealed an unlikely 1-0 victory and the club's first major trophy since 1935. The history-making side consisted of:

Chris Turner, Roland Nilsson, Phil King, John Harkes (Lawrie Madden), Peter Shirtliff, Nigel Pearson, Danny Wilson, John Sheridan, David Hirst, Paul Williams, Nigel Worthington (Unused sub: Trevor Francis)

After the celebrations died down the Owls were left with six games left to clinch promotion back to the top flight, still holding a four-point cushion over fourth-placed Millwall with three games in hand. In the end it was not Millwall that Wednesday had to fight off for the last promotion spot but Notts County as they surged from the chasing pack to pull to within five points with two games remaining. This meant Wednesday needed to beat Bristol City in their final home game and in front of almost 32,000 fans a brace from David Hirst, and a goal from Trevor Francis, started the celebrations in earnest as the Robins were beaten 3-1 to complete an outstanding return to the big time.

Second Division final table – 1990/91

		P	W	D	L	F	A	Pts
1	Oldham Athletic	46	25	13	8	83	53	88
2	West Ham United	46	24	15	7	60	34	87
3	WEDNESDAY	46	22	16	8	80	51	82
4	Notts County	46	23	11	12	76	55	80
5	Millwall	46	20	13	13	70	51	73
6	Brighton & HA	46	21	7	18	63	69	70

Not only was it a memorable season at first team level but the reserve side won the Central League title for the first time in thirty years and the youth side reached the final of the FA Youth Cup competition for the first, and only time.

WORST-EVER SEASON?

Like every club in the land, Wednesday have experienced their fair share of forgettable and traumatic seasons; such as the disastrous campaign of 1919/20 which ended in relegation from the top flight after just seven wins all season. However, the 1974/75 season must surely qualify as the worst in the club's history as Wednesday were at rock bottom, both on and off the field. The controversial sacking of Derek Dooley on Christmas Eve 1973 was roundly condemned by Owls fans and the team were then involved in a battle to stay in the Second Division – their status only assured on the final day of the 1973/74 season when Bolton Wanderers were beaten at Hillsborough. With the relatively inexperienced Steve Burtenshaw in the manager's post and fans in revolt after a large hike in season ticket prices – only 3,000 were eventually sold – optimism was in short supply for the new season and sadly this was well founded. With the club's finances also in a worsening state – their bank overdraft was increasing at an alarming rate – the season started badly and gradually deteriorated as just four wins before the dawn of 1975 left a low-scoring Owls side just one place off the foot of the division. Incredibly, from that moment until the end of the campaign, Wednesday did not win ANY of their final seventeen league games and were sadly relegated to the third tier, for the first time, after a 1-0 defeat at Nottingham Forest on April 1st 1975. The season set several unwanted club records with the Owls failing to score in eight consecutive home games, as well as also failing to score in eight consecutive away games. A run of five straight home defeats equalled the club record while the most astonishing record regarded the team's ability (or lack of) to find the net; from scoring at Fulham, in February 1975, Wednesday did not score again for 14 hours and 10 minutes! The crucial goal came in the final minute of the April 19th 1975 home game with Oxford United and this also meant it had been 14 hours and 25 minutes since the diehard fans had seen a home goal! Wednesday, of course, finished bottom of the Second Division, eleven points adrift, and the misery continued in 1975/76 as they finished in their worst-ever position – 20th in the Third Division. Incidentally, in the 2009/10 season the side equalled that club record of five consecutive home losses and failed to score for 10 hours and 31 minutes.

DON'T BET ON A 0-0 DRAW!

From the first-ever league meeting with Bury, in January 1896, Wednesday proceeded to score in every subsequent home game against the Lancashire club until a 0-0 draw on September 26th 1978 – a run of 34 games, spanning 82 years, eight months and four days! In fact, the clubs have only met at Hillsborough once more – Wednesday winning 5-1 in the 1979/80 season – with the Owls having won 23 times and drawn six of the 36 games.

CATALAN LEGEND

Dublin-born Irish international Patrick O'Connell appeared in 21 games for Wednesday just before the Great War. However, it was his exploits as a coach in Spain, between the wars, for which he is better known. He first made the almost unprecedented move into Spanish football in 1922, when he was appointed manager-coach at Racing Santander. After seven years in charge he spent five years at Atletico Madrid before winning the Spanish League title in 1935 during his only season in charge of Real Betis (then called Betis Balompie). He was appointed boss at FC Barcelona in 1936 but almost immediately a military coup signalled the start of the Spanish Civil War (1936-39) and O'Connell is widely regarded as the man who single-handedly steered the club through those turbulent times. He was at the helm when Barca won the Catalonian League and then the Mediterranean League before he took the club on a fundraising tour of Mexico and the United States in 1937. O'Connell was one of only four men from the 16-strong party that returned to war-torn Barcelona and, despite leaving in 1938, he managed in Spanish football until his retirement in 1958, leaving an indelible mark on the glorious history of FC Barcelona.

MOST LEAGUE POINTS

FA Premiership	64 points	1993/94
First Division	75 points	1991/92 (3 points)
	60 points	1929/30 (2 points)
Second Division/Championship	88 points	1983/84 (3 points)
	62 points	1958/59 (2 points)
Third Division/League One	72 points	2004/05 (3 points)
	58 points	1979/80 (2 points)

DRUNK IN CHARGE OF A FOOTBALL?

Almost forty years after Freddie Kean left Hillsborough for Bolton Wanderers, older Wednesday fans still talked about the day when the England international was supposedly drunk in the 6-2 home defeat to Blackpool on Christmas Day 1924. The half-back, who played in 247 games for the Owls, recollected the events many years later: "You know I've had to live with that for donkey's years. Even kids who weren't born at the time talk about it. Frankly, I had a stinker that day and I admit it, but some smart Alec said I must have been drunk – and the rumours swept Sheffield. They said I was loaded that day and in time everybody believed it. I was dropped for the return match at Blackpool, but everybody forgets that so were two or three others. But my wife will tell you that I hadn't had a drink. It's too soft to laugh at really." The rumours became so strong that Wednesday actually called a special inquiry that Kean attended. The Wednesday man wanted to know the name of the individual who said he had seen him drinking, so he could sue him, but Owls chairman Charles Clegg told Kean to; "Forget it, Kean. As far as we are concerned, it never happened." The Walkley-born player eventually settled back in Sheffield and worked as a publican for many years during which the drunk allegation remained a regular topic of conversation, much to Kean's annoyance!

NINE IN A ROW

The club record for scoring in consecutive games, rather unsurprisingly, belongs to Wednesday legend Derek Dooley who netted in nine games in a row during the memorable 1951/52 season:

27/10/51 v Queens Park Rangers	Away	2-2	1 goal
03/11/51 v Notts County	Home	6-0	5 goals
10/11/51 v Luton Town	Away	3-5	2 goals
17/11/51 v Bury	Home	2-1	2 goals
24/11/51 v Swansea Town	Away	2-1	2 goals
01/12/51 v Coventry City	Home	3-1	2 goals
08/12/51 v West Ham United	Away	6-0	3 goals
15/12/51 v Doncaster Rovers	Away	1-1	1 goal
22/12/51 v Everton	Home	4-0	4 goals

ONE HUNDRED YEARS AND COUNTING

In the early years of Wednesday's history the club called several grounds their home, including Highfields, Myrtle Road, Sheaf House and Hunter's Bar. For bigger games they hired Bramall Lane before in 1887 they took a lease on a piece of swampy land, which became their Olive Grove home for the next dozen years. The somewhat forced move to Owlerton occurred in 1899 and local rivals Chesterfield were the first visitors, on the opening day of the 1899/00 season. A healthy crowd of 12,000 attended the first match and quickly allayed fears that the move into the sparsely populated Owlerton district could spell the death knell for The Wednesday. The Lord Mayor kicked off that first match – on September 2nd 1899 – with newly relegated Wednesday represented by: Jimmy Massey, Jack Earp, Ambrose Langley, Bob Ferrier, Tommy Crawshaw, Herrod Ruddlesdin, Archie Brash, Jack Pryce, Harry Millar, Jock Wright, Fred Spiksley. It was visiting player Herbert Munday who scored the first goal at the new enclosure but Wednesday hit back to win 5-1 thanks to goals from Millar (2), Spiksley, Ferrier and Brash. Just over a hundred years later – on September 11th 1999 – Wednesday celebrated a century of football at Hillsborough when Everton visited S6 for a Premiership encounter. The Owls had made a terrible start to the season – having only one point to their name from the opening six games – and a crowd of 23,539 watched this record deteriorate further as first-half goals from Nick Barmby and Scott Gemmill took the Toffeemen to a 2-0 success. Fans who went through the turnstiles that day received a commemorative lapel badge while the matchday programme included a reprint of the first programme issued for a game at Hillsborough – in September 1901. In sharp contrast to the team that played in the first match, the side for the Everton game was truly multinational and included a Brazilian, Swede, Norwegian, Belgian and Italian and an unused Czech Republic goalie: Kevin Pressman, Peter Atherton, Ian Nolan, Des Walker, Emerson Thome, Niclas Alexandersson (Simon Donnelly 64), Danny Sonner, Lee Briscoe, Petter Rudi (Phil O'Donnell ht), Andy Booth, Gilles De Bilde (Benito Carbone). Subs not used: Jon Newsome and Pavel Srnicek.

LIVE TV

The first Wednesday match to be televised live from Hillsborough was the FA Cup quarter-final clash with Southampton on Sunday 11th March 1984. The somewhat dour game ended 0-0.

COMPENSATION

After the February 1906 FA Cup tie against Nottingham Forest, at Hillsborough, the club received two letters from Wednesday fans. A Mr Bird, from Attercliffe, wrote saying that he had ripped his coat on a rusty nail as he was coming through the turnstile and asked to be compensated for the accident. The second letter was also coat related as a Mr Wagstaff admitted that due to a lapse of memory he had left his coat on a nail at the Penistone Road end of the ground and also wanted to be reimbursed for his loss. Suffice to say, the Wednesday officials did not take too long in deciding to reject both appeals!

NICKNAMES

Norman Curtis	'Cannonball'
Harry Davis	'Joe Pluck'
David Layne	'Bronco'
Arthur Lowdell	'Darkie'
Ian Mellor	'Spider'
Albert Mumford	'Clinks'
Walter Millership	'Battleship'
John Pearson	'Bambi'
Darren Potter	'Harry'
Gary Shelton	'Stretch'
Mel Sterland	'Zico'
Kevin Taylor	'Ticker'
Charlie Tomlinson	'Shadow'
Cyril Turton	'Mother'
Danny Wilson	'Didwell'
Harry Woolhouse	'Toddles'
Nigel Worthington	'Irish'

RECORD HOME ATTENDANCES

The record attendance at Hillsborough is 72,841 for the FA Cup tie against Manchester City on February 17th 1934. The record Football League crowd is for the derby match against Sheffield United on January 5th 1952, when a crowd of 65,384 packed in to see the Blades win 3-1.

ROYAL VISIT

Her Majesty, Queen Elizabeth II has twice visited Hillsborough since she ascended to the throne in June 1953. Less than a year later, the young Queen visited Hillsborough where 40,000 schoolchildren packed into the ground to see the sovereign, on what was a rare visit to a domestic football ground. When secretary-manager Eric Taylor replied to her question about the origins of the club's name, she supposedly commented that "it is a very nice name". Over thirty years later, in December 1986, she visited Hillsborough for a very specific reason – the official opening of the newly roofed Kop. Over 40,000 people were inside Hillsborough on this occasion to see the monarch place the royal seal of approval on the much-awaited improvement to the traditional home end at the ground.

THIRD OLDEST

It is commonly thought that Sheffield Wednesday are the fifth oldest Football League club in England, behind Notts County, Stoke City, Nottingham Forest and Chesterfield. However, County's claim of 1862 has recently been called into doubt – historians now believing that 1864 would perhaps be more reasonable. Whichever year is used, they would still be the 'oldest league club' as Stoke City's claims of 1863 have long been discredited. In fact it has proven impossible to confirm any football activity in Stoke whatsoever before 1868, when a club named Stoke Ramblers came into being. To compound matters for the Potters, the original Stoke FC actually went bust in 1908! With Stoke demoted from second place it is left to Nottingham Forest to move up as their 1865 formation has long since been clarified as being correct – they were formed at a meeting in the Clinton Arms in that year. This would leave Chesterfield as the third oldest club but our Derbyshire neighbour's claim of 1866 is actually shot down in flames by their own website! The Spireites admit that the current club is probably the fourth to bear the town's name, with the first formed around 1867, after Wednesday's official date of formation. It is now thought that Chesterfield director, George Oram, exaggerated his club's formation, when writing a potted history of the club in 1905, to make sure they were older than their near neighbours Wednesday! As is often the case, this so-called fact was repeated through the years and still remains uncorrected to this day.

THE DRUGS DON'T WORK

Every professional player runs the risk, although slight, of receiving a career threatening injury when they step over the white line on a match day. For the vast majority, their careers will only be interrupted by relatively minor injuries but for some unfortunate players they do suffer the heartache of having to hang up their boots prematurely. In Victorian times, a simple broken leg could often spell the end for many players with Wednesday's George Lee having to retire from professional football after suffering a leg fracture in the FA Cup tie against Sheffield United, at Owlerton, in February 1900. The injury that ended the career of outstanding Wednesday and England player Billy Marsden was far more serious, leaving Marsden's life in danger after he was badly injured whilst playing for England against Germany in 1930. The game was the first full international between the two countries but was remembered for all the wrong reasons by Billy as an accidental collision with team-mate Roy Goodall left Marsden with horrific injuries; he suffered a broken neck and spinal damage. It was only the skill of a German surgeon that saved his life and one of Wednesday's finest-ever players spent several weeks in hospital before returning to England to begin his recuperation. Unfortunately, despite playing a handful of games for the reserve side, the injury spelt the end of his glittering career and after 221 games for the Owls, and three caps for his country, Marsden retired, receiving £750 compensation from the FA with Wednesday receiving almost three times as much (£2,000). The continued advances in modern medicine mean that a player can now recover from an injury, which half a century ago would have ended a career. Although still a serious injury, a modern-day player would not expect his career to be finished if he ruptured his cruciate knee ligament. Unfortunately, that was not the case back in the late 1940s when Wednesday man Eddie Kilshaw suffered the injury in an April 1949 game at Hillsborough, against Leicester City. The Owls had only splashed out £20,000 (£575,000 at today's prices) to Bury for his services the previous December. At the time, it was believed that he was the first player to have his ligaments sewn back together but the repair was in vain and in 1949 a medical report advised him against playing in 'serious football'. He finally accepted defeat in May 1951, hanging up his boots and starting a second career in teaching. The tragic events that ended with star 1950s forward Derek Dooley having his leg amputated have been well documented but in 1960 the club was again stunned when young reserve team player Doug McMillan suffered the same tragic fate. The

Owls were returning from a Boxing Day game at Arsenal when the team bus crashed on the A1, near Huntingdon. On an icy road the bus failed to navigate a double right-hand bend and Dougie was subsequently trapped in the wreckage. Sadly, the attending medical team had no choice but to amputate McMillan's leg, just below the knee, in order to free the 19-year-old and save his life. After adjusting to the life changing events, Wednesday held a benefit match for the youngster, over 25,000 attending a fundraising game between a Sheffield XI and a Select XI, the latter including Bobby Charlton and ex-Owl Albert Quixall. He was given an admin job at Hillsborough after the accident but would work for many years at a local bakery before taking over a sub-post office at Wincobank in 1972. He had made a victorious return to Hillsborough in 1968 when as manager of Hallam FC he watched his side win the Sheffield Senior Cup. Although the early retirement of Derek Wilkinson was no doubt a blow for the individual player he did at least enjoy over ten years of senior football before he was forced to end his career, aged 29, in 1965. The right-winger had joined from non-league football in 1952 and accrued 231 games for the Owls (57 goals) before he became dogged by a succession of niggling injuries. It was a persistent groin injury that finally forced his retirement with just over 10,000 fans attending his testimonial game in 1966. After leaving football he returned to his trade of French polishing and for 22 years, prior to his retirement in 2000, worked as a forklift truck driver in Stockport. Another player to benefit from a fundraising game was the unfortunate Paul Bradshaw who was forced into retirement, in October 1978, just over two years after signing from Burnley. The Owls beat Leeds United 4-2 in his benefit game at Hillsborough in September 1979. Bradshaw had already started his successful soccer schools, which ran until 1999. The uncle of ex-Owl keeper Matt Clarke succumbed to the inevitable due to a knee injury and played briefly in non-league football before retiring for good in 1981. It always seems worse when a highly promising young player is forced to pack in the game and this was the case with 1990s midfielder Ryan Jones. The 6 ft 1 in. central midfielder had made a big impression on the Wednesday fans, after breaking into the senior side in the memorable 1992/93 season. He quickly became a regular – winning a full cap for Wales thanks to a grandmother from the Principality – and was just one game short of 50 appearances for Wednesday when a serious ankle injury ended his Premiership career. He is still playing in Sheffield Sunday League football to this day. The early retirements of both Andy Hinchcliffe and Phil Scott were a massive financial blow to Wednesday at the time, both having signed lucrative contracts before being forced to quit the game. The former was signed by Ron Atkinson from Everton in 1998 – costing a £2.75m fee – and showed the undoubted quality that earned the left-back two full England caps whilst at Hillsborough. After the club were relegated in 2000 he only played a bit part in the final two years of his contract, appearing for only 17 minutes of the 2001/02 season, prior to retiring due to persistent knee problems in March 2002. Scottish midfielder Scott signed in March 1999 but in three years at Wednesday he started only three games, failing to make a single appearance for over two years before retiring in the summer of 2002. Ironically, after leaving the game, he worked as a fitness trainer! Fellow Scots Simon Donnelly and Phil O'Donnell both suffered horrendous injury problems during their time in Sheffield although the duo were not forced to retire, both returning to Scottish football where O'Donnell tragically passed away in December 2007, during the Motherwell versus Dundee United Scottish Premier Division fixture. Another young player whose career was cut short through injury was goalkeeper Chris Stringer. The rookie custodian had made his debut on the opening day of the 2000/01 season, when Kevin Pressman was sensationally sent off after 13 seconds, and performed heroics as the Owls grabbed a 1-1 draw at Wolves. Sadly, he then suffered a series of persistent injury problems, culminating in two blood clots on his thigh, which meant he gave in to medical advice in May 2004, after 12 games for the Owls. If his forced early retirement was not enough, he now cannot play football at all, due to deep vein thrombosis.

THE LIFE OF BRIAN

When appointed to the manager's position at Hillsborough on November 6th 2006, Brian Laws became the club's fifth boss since the Owls were relegated from the Premiership in 2000. Born in Wallsend, Tyne and Wear on October 14th 1961, Brian Simon Laws started his playing career as a trainee at Burnley, signing his first professional contract with the Lancashire club at the age of 17. After spells at Huddersfield Town and Middlesbrough he was signed by Nottingham Forest in 1988 with his new manager, Brian Clough, famously saying; "I've never seen you play, son, I'm going on the recommendation of Ronnie Fenton. So if you're crap, Ronnie signed you. If you're good, I signed you." Right-back Laws twice won the League Cup whilst with Forest – in addition to being a runner-up in the competition and the FA Cup – and appeared in 209 competitive games for the Nottingham club before signing for Grimsby Town in 1994. He was briefly player-manager at Blundell Park in the mid-1990s and following a short spell as a player at Darlington he began a long association with Scunthorpe United in 1997. His playing days ended at the Lincolnshire club and he duly led the Iron to promotion from the basement division in 1999 – United beating Leyton Orient 1-0 in the Wembley final. He was controversially sacked in March 2004, only to be re-instated three weeks later, and within twelve months earned promotion from League Two for a second time, Scunthorpe finishing runners-up to Yeovil Town. After nearly ten years at Scunthorpe he was appointed by Dave Allen at Hillsborough – much to the delight of his Wednesday supporting wife – with the former Owls chairman commenting; "I like him, he comes from the Clough camp, I'm a great admirer of the Clough camp." He hit the ground running at Wednesday, continuing the sterling work achieved by caretaker boss Sean McAuley, and playing some sparkling football his new club just missed out on reaching the Championship play-offs, after a terrific run of form. His honeymoon period came to a juddering halt at the start of the 2007/08 season as the highly personable Laws watched his side lose the first six games of the season! After a long hard campaign the club's status came down to the final game, at home to Norwich City, where in front of the biggest Championship crowd of the season – 36,208 – the Owls won 4-1 to save their skins. The 2008/09 campaign saw Wednesday finish firmly in mid-table although Laws achieved the feat that he probably will always be remembered for; being the first manager to take Wednesday to a double over Sheffield United for 95 years. There was genuine optimism that the Owls could push into the top ten of the Championship in the 2009/10 campaign but, after a bright start, the season deteriorated and Laws looked a dispirited man when his side meekly lost 3-0 at Leicester City on December 12th 2009. The defeat at the Walkers Stadium took the club's run of games without a win to nine and 24 hours later he left Hillsborough by 'mutual consent'. His overall record of 49 wins and 56 defeats, from 149 league games, was certainly not the worst record of the club's recent managers and it was noticeable that he remained a popular man with Wednesday fans throughout his tenure with supporters only showing signs of losing faith in what proved to be his final game in charge. Within a month of leaving Hillsborough, Laws was back in work when he was somewhat surprisingly appointed as manager at Premiership outfit Burnley, following Owen Coyle's move to Bolton Wanderers. Almost 17 years after leaving Turf Moor Laws returned – on a 2½ year contract – to be given his first shot at managing in England's top division.

INCOGNETIO

For a variety of reasons, several Wednesday players have made their debut for the club under an assumed name. This started way back in the 19th century with Harry Brandon, who played under the pseudonym of Todd in the first-ever meeting with Sheffield United, in December 1890. He was carried from the field by delighted Wednesday fans after a 2-1 win and within a few days was signed on a permanent basis. Another Wednesday player of the era, Jim Clarke, was bizarrely more commonly known by the name of Jim Smith – the goalie spending a decade in Wednesday colours prior to joining Rotherham County in 1893. The false name taken by the aforementioned Harry Brandon was simply so other clubs would not be alerted to his presence in Sheffield and this still holds true in modern times. Back in the pre-season of 1992, Wednesday met Maltby Miners Welfare in a friendly encounter and included a mystery goalkeeper in their squad. The man in question proved to be none other than Norwegian international Thomas Myhre. The former Everton and Glasgow Rangers custodian did not play for the Owls again but just over fours years later, in a second-team friendly at Stocksbridge Park Steels, the Owls gave a starting shirt to a player called Ryan Twerton. The stylish display of the new boy had Wednesday fans in the crowd speculating as to the real identity of the midfielder and it was soon disclosed as four days later the Owls paid £750,000 for the services of Orlando Trustfull from Dutch club Feyenoord. The Dutchman would spend only a season at Hillsborough with his 22 games split evenly between starting berths and substitute appearances. In the following season, travelling Owls fans were left scratching their heads when reserve-team midfielder Krystof Kotylo entered the fray from the substitutes' bench, in a testimonial match for Glasgow Rangers player Ian Durrant. The reason was that the man who ran onto the Ibrox pitch bore no resemblance whatsoever to Kotylo! It later transpired that is was new signing, Italian teenager Francesco Sanetti, who was guilty of identity theft as Wednesday had yet to be granted international clearance for the striker and were desperate to give the Roman a 'run out'. He duly made a goalscoring Premiership debut in the final home game of the season but sadly that was the highlight of his career in English football, Francesco returning home in June 1999 after just seven games for the Owls.

MONEY PIT

In March 1997, Wednesday announced plans to raise the princely sum of £17m through a 'placing and offer' share scheme. The involvement of London investment brokers Charterhouse Development Capital Funds was pivotal to the deal as they purchased £8.5m of the shares, as well as underwriting the remaining shares, which in turn were offered to existing shareholders at a price of 85p per share. The deal valued the club at £42.5m and gave the City of London financiers a 20% stake in Premiership Wednesday, with the stated intention of floating the club on the Stock Market within three years. All the monies raised were set to be spent on new players, improvements to the training, leisure and catering facilities and to reduce overall bank borrowings. The whole deal was swiftly put into action and in April 1997 Geoff Arbuthnott – a Charterhouse director – was appointed to the new Sheffield Wednesday plc board. To meet both FA and Stock Exchange rules the club split into two with the plc board becoming the parent company of its subsidiary Sheffield Wednesday Limited, the latter effectively running the club on a day-to-day basis. The whole scheme was subsequently ratified at an Extraordinary General Meeting (1,700 in favour and 100 against) and it was perhaps no coincidence that within four months of the deal being arranged the Owls broke their transfer record when signing Paolo Di Canio for £4.5m from Glasgow Celtic. The Owls also handed manager David Pleat a new contract, announced plans to replace the 13,000 wooden seats inside Hillsborough for the new plastic variety, and beat off competition to sign Peterborough 'wonderkids' David Billington and Mark McKeever. The new structure at the club also resulted in Ian Wood being appointed as Wednesday's first chief executive. However, hopes that the partnership would prove beneficial for both parties quickly started to fade as manager David Pleat was sacked in November 1997 and Wednesday spent all season at the wrong end of the top flight, before securing their status in the penultimate away game of the campaign. The club stabilised with a mid-table finish in 1999 but relegation in 2000 effectively ended any chance Charterhouse had of ever seeing a return on their initial investment. In January 2001 Arbuthnott resigned from the board of directors, with Wednesday struggling to avoid relegation from the second tier. The share capital held by Charterhouse was duly acquired by directors Keith Addy, Dave Allen and Geoff Hulley with approximately 9.45% being gifted to the Owls Trust.

FAIR PLAY

At the end of the 1999/2000 season the Owls were named as winners of England's 'fair play' award and were subsequently placed into a Uefa hat, along with 13 other teams, with two lucky clubs handed a place in the 2000/01 Uefa Cup tournament. Unfortunately, there was no good news to balance against the despair of relegation as sides from Spain and Belgium were drawn out to leave the Owls to concentrate on their first season outside of the top flight for a decade.

SAVED BY FOOTBALL

In modern football, it is now extremely rare for a player to spend his whole career with only one club. In Wednesday's history, dozens of players have spent over a decade on the Owls' books with the likes of Andrew Wilson and Tom Brittleton even spending two decades at Hillsborough. One player, though, remained a one-club man for a very special reason as full-back Willie Layton swore he would only play for Wednesday after he believed his life had been spared due to an Owls match! The incident occurred in November 1895 when Layton – a miner at Blackwell Colliery in Derbyshire – decided against working his usual night shift so he could be fresh for the Wednesday reserve game at Attercliffe on the following day. The Staffordshire-born player was hoping to secure a professional contract with Wednesday and his decision proved truly life saving as on the same night a massive underground explosion killed seven miners on the coal seam. From that day forth Layton swore to never play for another league side. In 14 years at Wednesday he totalled 361 games before creating a scandal in 1912 when he left his wife and children suddenly to emigrate to Australia!

FIRST IMPRESSION

Centre forward Ted Harper could not have wished for a better start to his Owls career, scoring a hat-trick on his debut in a 6-4 win at Derby County in November 1927. The attacker would score 16 times in just 22 games before moving to Spurs in March 1929 for £5,500 and remains the only Wednesday player to hit three goals in his first game in a blue and white shirt.

HAT-TRICK

Striker Luke Varney entered the club's record books when he signed on loan from Derby County in January 2010. He became the first player to have been signed on loan on three separate occasions, having made the temporary move in March and then August 2009.

PROGRAMME

A matchday programme first appeared in the city of Sheffield in 1897 when Sheffield United started to issue them. Before that date, both Sheffield teams had occasionally produced single cards, effectively containing just the date and teams, with Wednesday's oldest issue believed to be from the 1877 opening of Olive Grove. Wednesday started to produce their first 'proper' programme in their second season at Owlerton (1900/01) and have continued to this day, publishing for every league and cup game since.

PRISONER OF WAR

Goalkeeper Arnold Birch signed professional forms for Wednesday in 1917 but he was only able to do so after being allowed home to England, on compassionate grounds, from his internment in Holland. The Grenoside-born stopper had volunteered for the First Royal Naval Brigade in 1914 but after only a week stationed in Antwerp, the invading German army occupied the country and Birch's unit escaped to neutral Holland. Under the terms of international law, they were duly disarmed and detained in Holland, for what proved to be the duration of the war, and were eventually billeted in a specially-built barracks called 'The English Camp' in the town of Groningen. It was not long before the barracks formed their own football team and although banned from competing in official games, they played in a series of friendly matches against local Dutch teams. It was during these games that Birch – referred to as the 'English goalkeeper' – forged a big reputation and when he returned from his short visit to England he was signed by Dutch side Be Quick, making his official debut on February 3rd 1918. He later performed heroics in a 1-0 defeat to Ajax Amsterdam but left for Britain in November 1918 when the Great War ended. He would make 29 senior appearances for Wednesday while his time in Holland was recalled in a 2003 Dutch publication by historian Gerard Helsma; *Arnold Birch, the first professional footballer in Groningen.*

YOUTH CUP

The FA Youth Cup was introduced back in 1952 to give an opportunity for youth teams from both league and non-league sides to emulate their seniors by competing for a national trophy. Wednesday made a losing start in the competition – Hull City winning 3-2 at Hillsborough in September 1952 – before registering their first win just over a year later, 7-2 at Notts County. The early days of the tournament were dominated by the Manchester United youth team from which the legendary 'Busby Babes' would graduate. The Owls were thrashed by the United youth team 7-0 in February 1955 at Old Trafford but the 1956/57 season saw Wednesday reach the semi-finals for the first time, losing 2-0 on aggregate to West Ham United, after a crowd of 18,030 had seen Sheffield United beaten 1-0 in the Hillsborough quarter-final. The club's biggest win in the Youth Cup came in October 1961 when Stamford Youth Club lost 16-0 at Hillsborough (John Hickton scoring NINE) while Wednesday reached the last four again in 1963. Unfortunately, the terrible winter caused countless postponements and meant the semi-final was played as a one-off tie. After being forced to travel to Merseyside, Liverpool won 4-0 to knock the Owls out. The club then experienced many lean seasons and it was not until the outstanding youth side of the late 1970s that Wednesday again enjoyed a significant run. Victories over Bolton Wanderers, Wigan Athletic, Oldham Athletic and Wimbledon set up a meeting with Manchester City in the last eight. A goal from John Pearson secured a 1-1 result at home and City needed extra time at Maine Road before eventually winning the replay 3-2. The 2-0 loss at Bury in January 1982 saw both Simon Mills and David Mossman red carded, but in 1983 the Owls reached their third semi-final, beating Chelsea 4-2 to qualify. Unfortunately, Everton proved far too strong and after winning 2-0 in the Hillsborough first leg they completed a 9-0 aggregate win at Goodison Park.

Full Record (Inc. 2009/10)   P151 W71 D24 L56

Without doubt the Owls' finest moment in the competition came in the glorious 1990/91 season when the under-18 side equalled the feat of the senior side by reaching the cup final. After wins against Bury, Aston Villa, West Bromwich Albion and Hull City, Wednesday were drawn against Manchester United in the semi-final. The tie seemed to have swung towards the Lancashire club after the teams drew 1-1 in Sheffield but a dramatic last-minute own goal at Old Trafford handed Wednesday a 2-1 aggregate win and a place in their only FA Youth Cup final. The final proved to be a disappointment as Millwall won easily, 3-0, at Hillsborough in the first leg before the Owls restored some pride by gaining a 0-0 draw in London. Since reaching that final, Wednesday have struggled to make any real impact in the competition, with the 1998/99 season being the only occasion when they have reached the last sixteen, losing 3-1 in a replay to Everton. The club's most recent game proved a somewhat sobering experience as Sunderland won 7-2 at Hillsborough – Wednesday's worst-ever home loss in 57 years of Youth Cup football.

WIN OR LOSE

Between September 1960 and March 1973, the Owls faced Burnley on 24 occasions in league football without drawing once – Wednesday winning on 11 occasions and the Turf Moor club 13. The Owls' 7-0 win in May 1967 was a definite highlight for fans of the blue and white persuasion.

DIDN'T HAVE THE FOGGIEST

Former Wednesday goalkeeper Richard Siddall made the national press in December 2002 when he was left standing in goal when a Stocksbridge Park Steels v. Witton Albion game was abandoned after 30 minutes due to dense fog. He was named 'Clown of the Week' on BBC Radio's Mark and Lard afternoon show and the story gained several column inches in the tabloids, particularly after Barnsley-born Siddall admitted that he was literally 'in the dark' for about two minutes before a couple of visiting Witton fans told him the game had been abandoned! The goalie had been signed by Wednesday as cover near the end of the 2001/02 season and was an unused sub on five occasions before returning to non-league football.

BIG FOOT

When Wednesday signed Scottish goalkeeper Bill Allan in December 1891 they found they did not have boots big enough for him! A local cobbler worked through the night, allowing Allen to make his debut the following day!

TEENAGE KICKS

It is now almost 40 years since goalkeeper Peter Fox entered the record books as the Owls' youngest-ever player. An injury crisis had resulted in manager Derek Dooley being without both of his senior men – Peter Springett and Peter Grummitt – and he had no choice but to put apprentice Fox between the posts for the Second Division home game against Orient on March 31st 1973. Aged just 15 years, 8 months and 26 days, the teenager coped admirably on his big day and managed to keep a clean sheet as Wednesday won 2-0 thanks to goals from Brian Joicey and David Sunley. After his eventful day it was back to apprentice duties for the youngster – who was nursing a broken toe from his senior debut – and he would play over 20 senior games for the Owls before signing a professional contract, in June 1975. After 52 appearances for the club he recorded over 400 games for Stoke City and is now employed as a goalkeeping coach. The record for the youngest top-flight appearance by a Wednesday player is currently held by Mark Platts, who made his debut as a sub, against Wimbledon at Hillsborough in February 1996, aged just 16 years and 263 days. The exciting left-winger joined the Owls at the tender age of just eight and was a real star in junior football – appearing for England boys at Wembley – and enjoyed a meteoric rise through the ranks to make his Premiership bow whilst still a YTS trainee. He replaced Chris Waddle, with five minutes remaining, in his debut game and made a second appearance from the bench two weeks later. Sadly, though, that was the sum of his time in the spotlight, Platts dropping back into the reserves. He even briefly returned to Northern Intermediate League football, despite having turned professional along with Steve Haslam, in October 1996, and his fall from grace was complete when he attended a two-week trial at Sheffield United(!). He subsequently moved to Torquay United on a full transfer in March 1999 and appeared in 41 matches for the Devon club before returning home to Sheffield, where he played alongside Chris Waddle for Worksop Town. Within a few months he decided to retire altogether and now works in the construction industry with all his early promise just a distant memory. Although Platts still holds the record as the club's youngest top-flight player, he was pushed into second place overall in August 2006 when Academy scholar Matt Bowman appeared as a substitute, in a League Cup tie against Wrexham at Hillsborough, aged just 16 years and 205 days. The Barnsley-born player therefore beat Platts' record by 58 days although his appearance in the embarrassing 4-1 defeat proved to be his only senior game for the club as he was released in 2008 after failing to secure a professional contract.

ESCAPE FROM GERMANY

Inter-war Wednesday hero Billy Marsden had a lucky escape in May 1940 when he was trapped in Holland, as the invading Germans started their occupation of the country. Since injury ended his career in 1930, Billy had coached in Dutch football, but he and his wife were forced to leave all their possessions behind and literally flee for their lives. He sought refuge in a barber's shop and later recounted that there were 12 other men in the shop, but "no-one wanted a shave, however".

SHIPWRECKED!

Defender William Collier, who signed for Wednesday from Raith Rovers in 1924, had reason to remember his club's 1923 tour of the Canary Islands; the Raith team's ship ran aground off the coast of northern Spain! The vessel, bound for Argentina, was engulfed by a violent storm and after it became grounded on a sandbank near Corruedo it was everybody overboard! Thankfully, a fishing boat rescued all the passengers and after a few days in emergency accommodation the squad were able to complete their journey on a passing cruise liner.

GETTING SHIRTY

Mainly due to the opinions of various referees, the Owls have on several occasions, in recent years, been forced to wear an alternative kit to the one that was originally intended. It was down to the official in the December 1990 game against Notts County, at Hillsborough, when he decided that neither of the visitors' two playing strips – black and white stripes or pale blue – did not clash with the Owls' home kit. Wednesday fans were therefore treated to the unusual sight of seeing their side playing at home in their yellow and blue away kit! It was Wednesday's away kit which was deemed unsuitable in September 2000 for the First Division game at Tranmere Rovers. Owls assistant manager Peter Shreeves actually spoke to match referee Ray Oliver in the days leading up to the game to make sure Wednesday would be OK to play in their home kit, but just 30 minutes before kick-off he changed his mind! Therefore, Wednesday had no choice but to wear a very fetching ensemble of purple socks, black shorts and Tranmere's green away shirt!

TAXI FOR MR CARBONE

When David Pleat paid a club record £3m fee – to Inter Milan in October 1996 – for Italian attacker Benito Carbone he bought a highly talented, but also highly volatile, player; unlike his fellow countryman Paolo Di Canio who was calmness personified! After delighting the Hillsborough crowd for two seasons, scoring some superb goals in the process, he first found himself in hot water in the summer of 1998 when arriving back late from Italy for the start of pre-season training. In fact, Wednesday were already playing a series of warm-up games and his appearance in a late July match at Lincoln City was so well received by the travelling Owls fans that the problem subsequently melted away. However, just over a year later came an infamous game at The Dell, Southampton when Owls manager Danny Wilson dropped Benny to the bench as the club tried to stop of run of poor results which had seen Wednesday slip to the bottom of the Premiership. The Italian simply refused to take the subs' bench and quickly left the ground and subsequently flew straight home! Two weeks later he was on the bench for the home game with Everton and then made an early substitute appearance in the disastrous 8-0 drubbing at Newcastle United. By this time his popularity with Wednesday fans was at an all-time low and it was no surprise when the two sides parted acrimoniously in October 1999 with Carbone joining Aston Villa for a nominal £250,000 fee, after 26 goals in 107 games for the Owls. He later played Premiership football for Bradford City, Derby County and Middlesbrough before returning home to play for Como, Parma and Catanzaro. He also spent a month with Australian club Sydney FC in October 2006 before signing for Italian minnows AC Pavia in August 2007. The little club – based 35km south of Milan – have never played in the Italian top division and were last in the second tier (Serie B) over 50 years ago. In front of three figure crowds, Carbone is a big fish in a little pond and his presence has attracted much welcome publicity for the little-known side. His two outstanding goals on the final day of the 2008/09 Lego Pro Seconda Divisione helped Pavia to avoid the drop into the regional leagues and between spells out of the side through injury he continues to be an unlikely focal point in the depths of the Italian Football League.

SUBSTITUTE

Graham Hyde has made the highest number of substitute appearances in senior games, coming off the bench 54 times; Trevor Francis is second in the list with 51 sub appearances.

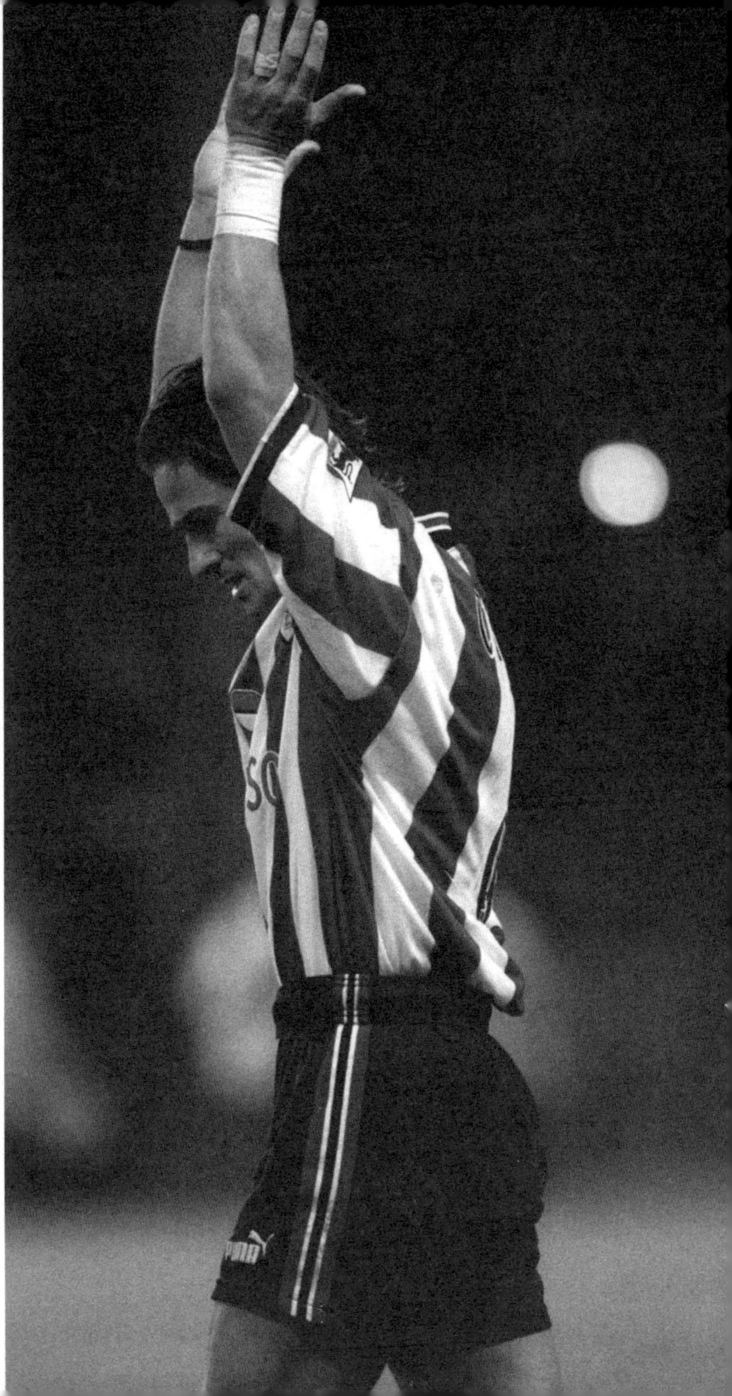

ENIGMATIC ITALIAN BENITO CARBONE

BIGGEST DERBY GAME

Although the two city clubs have met on numerous occasions, in a variety of competitions, there is no doubt that the most high-profile clash came in the semi-final of the FA Cup in April 1993. Both Sheffield sides had drawn their sixth round games and knew before kicking off in their respective replays that the draw had thrown up a possible meeting in the last four. The Blades duly beat Blackburn Rovers on penalties, after a 2-2 draw, and then a goal from Paul Warhurst, against Derby County at Hillsborough, ensured two derby games in the semi-finals with Tottenham having drawn Arsenal. The FA immediately scheduled the London derby for Wembley but sent the two Sheffield teams up the M1 to Elland Road. That decision caused a public outcry in Sheffield and within 24 hours the FA had bowed to public pressure – moving the Steel City clash to Wembley on Saturday 3rd April with a 1pm kick off. Preparations then began in earnest for the biggest-ever migration of Sheffield football fans out of the city with match tickets selling out quickly. A crowd of 75,364 was inside Wembley to see the long-awaited tie but the red and white half of the city was stunned after 62 seconds when Chris Waddle fired home a spectacular long-range effort! Despite constant pressure from Wednesday, the Blades equalised through Alan Cork (looking not too dissimilar to Captain Birdseye after he had sworn not to shave until their cup run came to an end!). The game duly went into extra time where a downward header from Mark Bright sealed a 2-1 win for the Owls to clinch their second domestic cup final appearance for the season. Sadly both were lost – to a somewhat negative Arsenal side – but the 1992/93 season had still been one for fans to remember with the win over the Blades the definite highlight.

SUPERSTITIOUS

Lucky mascots have always been prevalent and footballers are not immune from their own superstitions. Legendary Wednesday winger Ellis Rimmer was particularly superstitious and on a matchday always had in his possession a horseshoe decorated with a black cat. However, before the 1935 FA Cup Final, against West Bromwich Albion, he suddenly realised that he had left the item back in the Hillsborough dressing rooms! He immediately thought he would be unable to maintain his record of scoring in every round prior to the final. Unbeknown to Rimmer, though, was that trainer Sam Powell had found the lucky charm and it arrived at Wembley just after half-time – Rimmer spookily scoring twice after its arrival as Wednesday lifted the cup!